Apostle to Zaire

The Life and Legacy of Blessed
Father Cosmas of Grigoriou

HIEROMONK COSMAS GRIGORIATIS
1942 - 1989

Be thou faithful unto death, and I will give thee a crown of life.
Revelation 2:10

APOSTLE TO ZAIRE

The Life and Legacy of Blessed
Father Cosmas of Grigoriou

Demetrios Aslanidis &
Monk Damascene Grigoriatis

Preface by
Archimandrite George
Abbot of Grigoriou Monastery
Mount Athos

UNCUT MOUNTAIN PRESS

APOSTLE TO ZAIRE

Copyright 2001, 2022
Uncut Mountain Press

All rights reserved. This book may not be reproduced, in whole or in part, including illustrations, in any form without permission from the publisher.

uncutmountainpress.com

Cover Photo: Blessed Father Cosmas among the children of the Kolwezi Mission in Zaire.
Back Cover Photo: Students of the Light of Christ School, which was founded by Father Cosmas.

All Scriptural quotations are taken from the King James Version, unless otherwise noted. The translator to better reflect the original Greek text has emended some quotations.

This translation has been made from the Greek editions of the works entitled Ο Ιεραπόστολος του Ζαϊρ Π. Κοσμάς Γριγοριάτις by Demetrios Aslanidis and Μέγας Ει, Κύριε, και Θαυμαστά τα έργα σου: Αληθινές Ιστόριες από την Ιεραπόστολη στην Αφρική by Monk Damascene Grigoriatis, both published by the missionary association *Agios Kosmas Aitolos*, Thessaloniki.

Library of Congress Cataloging-in-Publication Data
Apostle to Zaire—2nd ed.
Written by Demetrios Aslanidis & Monk Damascene Grigoriatis

ISBN: 978-1-63941-010-1

I. Orthodox Christianity
II. Orthodox Christian Missions

To all those who, for the love of Christ and their fellow man, "hate their life in this world" and live for the preaching of the Gospel of Peace and the upbuilding of Christ's most Holy Church.

"The missionary's beginning is significant, however it is not the sum of the matter. . . The outset might be blessed or might become blessed at the end. What's important is that the giving be true and total, without holding back, with a disposition to self-sacrifice and self-denial, and with the aim of leaving our bones among the natives."

Blessed Father Cosmas Grigoriatis
From *Thoughts about Missionary Work from Experience*

CONTENTS

Preface to the First Greek Edition
by Archimandrite George
Abbot of Grigoriou Monastery, Mount Athos 12

Introduction to the English Edition
by Fr. Peter Alban Heers 15
 A Model of Mission in the Age of Antichrist **16**
 An Ascetic First **18**
 Exactness in Orthodoxy **20**
 Basic Presupposition: Working Under the Local Bishop **24**
 A Visionary who took One Step at a Time **26**
 A Fruit-bearing Tree for Generations to Come **28**

Book I
The Life of Blessed Father Cosmas
by his father, Demetrios Aslanidis 35
 Birth and Upbringing **35**
 Studies **37**
 Life in the Church **38**
 Technical School and Other Pursuits **39**
 Military Service **41**
 The Brotherhood of the Holy Cross and Other Studies **41**
 The First Period of the Mission **48**
 Return to Greece **51**
 At the Holy Monastery of Gregoriou **52**
 The Second Mission Period **56**
 The Spiritual Education of the Africans **58**
 The Farm and Stock-Raising Facilities **62**
 The Mission Churches in the Kolwezi Region **64**
 Journeys in Greece **65**
 The Mission Staff at Kolwezi **68**

Contents

How the Mission Worked **69**
The Facilities and Properties of the Mission **72**
Love of His Fellow Man **75**
Duties of Judge and Shepherd **78**
Samba, the African Doctor **80**
The Mission Workshops **81**
Catechism, Baptism and Marriage **82**
Liturgical Life and Tours of the Missionaries **86**
Translations into Swahili **89**
The Recognition of Orthodoxy **90**
Bitter Experiences and Trials **92**
His Sudden End **94**

Epilogue
The Last Days of Blessed Father Cosmas
by his trusted co-worker, Basil Berberi   101
    Friday, January 20, 1989 **102**
    Friday, January 27, 1989 **103**
    Monday, January 30, 1989 **105**

Afterword
In Praise and Memory of Blessed Father Cosmas
by His Eminence Bishop Avgoustinos,
former Metropolitan of Florina, Greece   107

Afterword II
In Praise and Memory of Blessed Father Cosmas
by Archimandrite Ioanikios Kotsonis
St. Gregory Palamas Monastery, Thessaloniki   111

Extracts from:
The Letters of Blessed Father Cosmas   117
    Arrival and Beginnings **117**
    Like the New Testament **122**

The Love and Support of the Monastery **124**
The Power of the Blessed Baptismal Waters **127**
Hope Not in Men but in the Lord of the Mission **129**
The Struggle will be a Long One **131**
The Problem of Ordinations **133**
Pentecost Yesterday, Today and Forever **135**
Pastoral Discernment **137**

Extracts from:
The Book of Blessed Father Cosmas
Thoughts about Missionary Work from Experience   141
   The Place of Action **141**
   The Human Dynamic **142**
   The Means and Manner of Evangelism **143**
   From the Countryside to the Center **144**
   From the Center to the Countryside **145**
   Philanthropy **146**
   The Life of Worship **146**
   Challenges to Evangelism **147**
   Syncretism **147**
   Today's Colonialism **149**
   The Role of Orthodoxy **149**

Orthodoxy and Magic on the Black Continent
An interview with Blessed Father Cosmas   151

Book II
The Legacy of Blessed Father Cosmas
by Monk Damascene Grigoriatis   157

Reflections on, and Incidents from the Life of
Blessed Father Cosmas   157
   Help Provided to Travelers **157**
   Journeys on Swampy Roads **159**

Parish Feasts **159**
Flee from Magicians **160**
The Authorities' Respect for Father Cosmas **160**
Translation Work at the Mission Center **161**
The Pilgrimage Site and Oil Lamp of Father Cosmas **162**
The Schools Run by the Orthodox Mission **163**
Father Cosmas' Declaration After Death **166**
Father Cosmas Demands the Return of the Flask **166**
Urged to Continue Catechism **166**
The Children at the Boarding School Told Us … **167**
Zairian Priests Told Us… **167**
Father Cosmas' Intercession Heals Sub-deacon Seraphim **167**

INCIDENTS AND ACCOUNTS OF WITCHCRAFT 169
"He is Greater than Me" **169**
The Vicious Circle of Demonocracy **169**
Deceived by the Love of Money **173**
The Orthodox Priest is a Fire to the Sorcerer **176**
Powerless Before the Power of God **178**
The Decisive Blow **179**
A Young Sorcerer Comes to the Light **179**
The Refusal to Surrender His Magic Objects **180**
The Sad Departure of a Roman Catholic Missionary **181**
A Protestant Missionary Receives a Teaching **182**

MIRACLES, MISSIONARY WORK AND SIGNS FROM THE SAINTS 185
We Want the Apolytikion of Saint Patapios **185**
Go to the True Church where Priests Have Beards & Cassocks **186**
A Roman Catholic is Led to the True Church **187**
The Dove and the Glimmering Flame **188**
"Your Faith Has Made You Well" **189**
A Young Girl is Brought Back to Life **189**
An Idol-worshipping Woman **190**
"Not this Way . . . There is a Church there" **191**

A Boarding School Student told us... **192**
Theft at the Parish of Saint Theodore **192**
Spiritual Advice **193**
Our Saints are with Us in All Circumstances **193**
Healed by Saint Theodore **194**
Healed of Sterility **194**
The Child Should Die in Church **195**
A Stroke of Lightning **195**
An Outbreak of the Measles **195**
Miraculous Protection **196**
Protected from Cholera **196**
How do you Orthodox Pray? **197**
Seek First the Kingdom of God... **198**
Someone in a Cassock Enters the Church **199**
Saint David Walks in the Tent **200**
A Miraculous Conversion **201**
A Miraculous Intervention **202**
A Miraculous Visit **202**
I saw the Panagia Theotokos **202**
A New Saul Comes into the Church **203**
Double Healing of an Anemic Girl **207**
The Archangel Michael in Kolwezi **207**
A Miracle of Ss. Nektarios and Anastasia **209**
Sacred Artifacts Rescued from Fire **210**
Go to the Orthodox Church **211**
Our Orthodox Faith Reaches Distant Sandoa **212**
Adventures in Pastoral Work **213**
Better to be Poor and Orthodox than Rich and Heretical **214**
Better to be Poor and Orthodox than Rich and Muslim **214**

Baptismal Testimonies   216

The Missionary Association of St. Cosmas Aitolos   223

The Holy Monastery of Grigoriou, Mount Athos

PREFACE
To the First Greek Edition

by Archimandrite George
Abbot of Grigoriou Monastery, Mount Athos

The 27th January 1991 saw the second anniversary of the death of our late brother, Hieromonk Cosmas Gregoriatis, the *Ierapostolos* (missionary) of Zaire.

Time has not made us forget, as is the usual case. On the contrary, his memory remains green in the souls of many people, and new writings are being published about his life and work.

We deemed it a duty to publish the present volume which contains: a) the life of Fr. Cosmas, told with simplicity and authenticity by his father, Demetrios Aslanides, a man who more than makes up in charm what he lacks in book-learning and b) an anthology of letters which in part refers to his missionary struggle.

Both his biography and his letters help us understand better the personality of Fr. Cosmas, his virtues, the difficulties he encountered, his faith in Christ, his Church life and his fighting spirit. They are consoling, constructive, chastening and enlightening texts. Texts written from pain and therefore genuine, authentic and true, just as are the teachings of Cosmas Aitolos, the memoirs of Makryiannis and the New Martyrology of Saint Nikodemos the Athonite.

Texts stamped with the sacrifice and blood of Fr. Cosmas.

Texts which are guides for modern missions.

I thank God for bringing Fr. Cosmas to our Holy Monastery and accounting us worthy to assist him, however humbly, in his struggle.

Now Fr. Cosmas is at rest in the land of the living and prays for us and his beloved Africans, to whom he gave his whole life and his mortal remains.

Pray also for us, Fr. Cosmas our much-loved child in Christ that, weak as we are, we may be counted worthy of the struggle and that we may meet in the eternal Kingdom of the Holy Trinity.

Archimandrite George
Abbot of the Holy Monastery of
Gregoriou* on the Holy Mountain

---

* Editor's note: "Gregoriou" appears variously in this book as "Gregoriou," "Grigoriou," and "St. Gregory."

BLESSED FATHER COSMAS GRIGORIATIS
1942 - 1989

INTRODUCTION
To the English Edition

By Fr. Peter Alban Heers

> *Being perfected in a short time, he fulfilled long years;*
> *for his soul was pleasing to the Lord.*
>
> — Wisdom of Solomon 4:13

In every generation there are those few exceptional souls who rise out of the conventionality of social life to become pathfinders to the catholicity and otherworldliness of Christianity. Heroic and uncompromising, they imitate Abraham and become exiles and martyrs for Christ, following Him with loving exactness and mountain-moving faith. They "hate their life in this world" in order to keep it – and that of their neighbor's – for eternity; and to successive generations they become models to imitate, witnessing, long after their departure, to the honour the Father bestows on those who serve Him.

Such a one was Blessed Father Cosmas of Grigoriou, enlightener of Zaire.

A Model of Mission in the Age of Antichrist

From as early as eighteen years of age he received from God the call to work in His mission field. Possessed of a dynamic personality that was "inspired by a burning love for Christ, he did not want to live a conventional Christian life nor to be limited to some usual ecclesiastical career and service. He longed to offer himself entirely to God and his fellow man."[1] He sought not honors, for "his chief concern was with the salvation of men and the upbuilding of Orthodoxy in Zaire."[2] The beloved Cosmas was, in the words of the former Metropolitan Avgoustinos of Florina, "the trailblazer of a beautiful journey for our race." He made Christ's departing directive to "teach all nations" his point of departure from a life of compromise and port of entry for Orthodoxy in the sub-Saharan and the hearts of countless souls. Unlike missionaries of heterodox confessions, he laid stress on both the first and second part of the Great Commission: "Go ye therefore, and teach all nations, baptizing them in the name of the Father, and of the Son, and of the Holy Spirit; teaching them to observe all things whatsoever I have commanded you." His success, or rather faithfulness, in carrying out the first half of the Great Commission,[3] was a direct result of his faithfulness and resolute determination to observe the second half, that is, to be exact in teaching them "to observe all things" that Christ has commanded us.

It could not be otherwise, for the African resembles neither the contemporary European, worn out by centuries of dizzying ideologies and spent on a myriad of humanistic philosophies, nor the typical American, quick to compromise and moderate things in order to achieve outward success. His noble, humble soul still inclines toward the other world and his simple, intuitive mind still has a healthy disposition for the noetic realm. A few months before his departure from this life, Father Cosmas

---

1 Archimandrite George of Grigoriou, *Ierapostolos of Zaire, Father Cosmas Grigoriatis*, St. Cosmas Aitolos Missionary Association, Thessaloniki, 1996, p. 160.

2 Ibid, p.161.

3 Fr. Cosmas baptized more than 15,000 souls in his 12 years of service to the Church in Zaire.

visited the monastery of his repentance and spoke to the pilgrims there of this African nobility and their desire for authentic, ascetic Orthodoxy. Bishop Athanasios Yievtich, a close disciple of the great contemporary Church Father, Archimandrite Justin Popovich, was present and relates what Fr. Cosmas had to say:

"They are people with a sensitivity and awareness of the inner world. Europeans usually underestimate them, but they are very mistaken. The soul of the African inclines toward mysticism and for this reason Orthodoxy has something to say to them and something to offer, but only authentic Orthodoxy – monastic, hagiorite Orthodoxy. For among the brethren of Africa, witchcraft and magic holds great sway, a real demonocracy. In Africa, I saw how true the Gospel of Christ is! Everything that He said about the possession of men by the demons, I saw first hand. However, the Living and True God is more powerful than Satan and all his servants. Let it be understood, however, that true missionary-apostolic work cannot be carried out in Africa if one does not decide to leave one's bones there."[4]

And so, in teaching the native Africans the entire Gospel of Christ and revealing to them the undistorted Image of the God-Man and His Church, it was only to be expected that his self-offering would likewise be complete and unqualified. In his "unique, genuine and very useful"[5] study on mission work, entitled *Thoughts about Missionary Work from Experience*, he lays out the cornerstone principle for all who would follow his example:

"The missionary's beginning is significant, however it is not the sum of the matter . . . The outset might be blessed or might become blessed at the end. What's important is that the giving be true and total, without holding back, with a disposition to self-sacrifice and self-denial, and with the aim of leaving our bones among the natives..."[6]

---

4 Bishop Athanasios Yievtich, *Hieromonk Cosmas the Hagiorite, Praboslabie* (newspaper), Patriarchate of the Orthodox Church of Serbia, #530, 1989, p. 15.
5 Archimandrite George, *Ierapostolos*, p. 160
6 Cosmas Grigoriatis, *Thoughts about Missionary Work from Experience*, Brotherhood of Foreign

Long before he leaves his bones on the mission field, however, he must have first discarded his pride and vainglory, if he wants the final offering to be fruitful. Thus, for Fr. Cosmas, the true missionary, in order to attain the blessed end, must leave no room for jealousy or vainglory, but rather must understand that all is to be shared: "common the struggle, common the pain, and common the glory of the Church."[7] He must "offer an open heart, love and communicate with others, concern himself with his own problems without adding more; being attentive to what others are doing, without turning to the devil and causing division."[8] And carrying out his duty in humility, "the true missionary does not seek recognition for his work, neither from the natives nor from those abroad, for the testimony of his sound conscience and the witness of his spiritual father and co-workers is sufficient for him."[9]

An Ascetic First

Father Cosmas left no room to doubt that he followed his principles, that his words were based on experience and his beginning and end were blessed. All of this is based on the fact that he "was first of all an ascetic and afterwards a missionary," as Archimandrite Ioanikios has written elsewhere in this book. He knew from experience what asceticism, fasting, vigil and prayer mean for the Church. "We thank the Lord," writes his Abbot George, "for, even if he was a man like us, he nevertheless disdained the earthly, the fleshly comforts, the human pleasures, all for the love of Christ, and chose a road that was harsh, combative, extremely tiring and humanly punishing. He did all of this for the love of God, his brothers and fellow men."

Orthodox Mission, Thessaloniki, 1988, pgs. 7-8.

7 *Thoughts about Missionary Work from Experience*, p. 9.

8 Ibid.

9 Ibid.

Elder George further certifies all this with a story from Father Cosmas' early days at the monastery: "I once passed by Fr. Cosmas' little cell and saw his bed: wooden boards and on top of the boards, a little thin sheet. He didn't even have a blanket. Having seen that, and other things, I thought that the brother had the grace of God and ought to become a monk."[10]

His asceticism, however, was not reserved to sleeping on wooden boards or even to fasting, vigil and prayer. Father Cosmas was above all unrelenting in his work of building up the Church in Zaire. Father Michael Christodoulidis of Cyprus writes of his visit to the Kolwezi mission and Father Cosmas' asceticism in work:

"That which distinguished him most was his industry and diligence in work, his method and organization of labor, his intelligence, speed and facility in confronting difficulties, his ingenuity, and his unshakeable faith, spirit of love and sacrifice . . . Untiring in work, he would labor long hours in every kind of task. We didn't know what midday was and what lunch means. The table of the Mission center is set from noon until late in the evening. Work 'from the morning watch until night' on roads that are non-existent, with vehicles and machines that were always breaking down, with bloody sacrifices, 'in afflictions, in necessities, in distresses, in wounds, . . . in labors, in vigils' (2 Cor. 6:4-5)."[11]

The above description not only finds repeated confirmation in a number of similar testimonies, but from the words of Father Cosmas himself, who at the same time points us to another aspect of his giving of priority to asceticism. He writes the following:

"It is well known that we all work here on a twenty four hour basis, under poor conditions, with the consequence being bodily strain and spiritual slackening. Consequently, toward the realization of spiritual and bodily replenishment, the existence of two monasteries, one men's and

---

10 Archimandrite George of Grigoriou, speech given the day after the sudden death of Fr. Cosmas, Saturday, February, 28, 1989, at the Metochian of the Holy Monastery of Grigoriou, Stavroupoli, Thessaloniki.
11 Fr. Michael Christodoulidis, *O Ierapostolos, Foreign Missions* (journal), #113, 1989, pgs. 209-217.

one women's, at some distance from the mission base, is deemed most appropriate . . . The monastery would work strictly as a monastery or, with the blessing of the local Metropolitan, as a Metochian (dependency) of Mount Athos, without any entangling with the mission."[12]

It was because Father Cosmas believed that a local Church could not stand without monasticism that he gave priority to the founding of a monastery and, towards the end of his life, he finally saw the realization of his plans with the establishment of the holy women's Monastery of St. Nektarios.

Exactness in Orthodoxy

Shortly after Fr. Cosmas' repose, upon seeing the spiritual labor he had accomplished, his successor Father Meletios said: "Father Cosmas' work in Africa is quite extensive. I found the whole Athonite typikon in place in Zaire. The Christians with prayer ropes in their hands. In church they chant all together lead by the choir of boys. No one communes without first having confessed. They keep strictly the fasts of Wednesday and Friday. They celebrate daily the Divine Services of Matins, Vespers and Small Compline. And on Sundays the congregation exceeds four hundred."[13]

Many have commented: "How is it that the Africans, being only recently baptized, can maintain such an intensity and exactness in their Orthodoxy, while many of us in parishes in Greece, America and elsewhere are much more lax?" The answer, I believe, lies partly in that Father Cosmas, their father, guide, and example, was himself strict and precise in his living and imparting of Orthodoxy. He was a monk in the long tradition of Athonite monasticism, and he hailed from

---

[12] *Thoughts about Missionary Work from Experience*, p. 11.

[13] Archimandrite George of Grigoriou, *Reflections on the Contribution of Athonite Monasticism to the Missionary Work of the Church, Synaxis* (journal), #78, April–June 2001, p. 98

the city of Ss. Cyril and Methodios, Thessaloniki, known for its rich ecclesiastical tradition. He kept with *exactness*, as well as discernment, the canons and standards of the Church, not out of some kind of reactionary conservatism or unfeeling zeal, but out of humility and because they provide what is best for man's soul, derived as they are from the experience and wisdom of the Saints and Fathers of the Church.

One such issue, in which he consciously chose the blessing of God's Saints over the transient benefits of our ecumenical age, was baptism. "When baptizing," he says, "I implement the Athonite order of things. We've done 250 baptisms, and, not only with idol worshippers, but also with Catholics who become Orthodox, we baptize them in deep rivers. My actions will have consequences when news reaches the Patriarchate of Alexandria, which holds that the Protestants are only in need of chrism. Until then, however, we will only do baptisms so as to have St. Nicodemos' blessing."[14]

Father Cosmas, as is clear further down, was not one to fly in the face of ecclesiastical authority. His decision to baptize those coming from heterodox confessions was done purely out of love for their souls and their eternal salvation, as well as love for God and His Saints, not suffering his conscience to disobey their sacred teachings. He acted not only out of respect for the Saints of ages past, but out of humility and obedience to the wise counsels of living saints: "I remember the words of Father Paisios, who told me that, most of the time, the baptism that the heretics perform only passes over their skin."[15] Having this in mind, his love for the catechumens dictated that he provide them with the complete and saving initiation into the eternal life of the Church. This had consequences, of course, but not only for his relationship with the upper hierarchy. Primarily it had consequences for the establishment of a spiritually healthy, powerful and faithful Orthodox Church, before which the Orthodox world now stands in admiration.

---

14 See the Letter entitled *Like the New Testament* on page 122.
15 *Thoughts about Missionary Work from Experience*, p. 21.

Mission central: sacred chant, catechism, priestly formation.

Similarly, Father Cosmas' success in establishing a strong, stable and healthy Orthodox way of life among the natives is also due to his refusal to adopt non-Orthodox methods and manners. Father Cosmas writes, "It is wrong to have recourse to the means and methods of the heterodox. Let us leave to Orthodoxy her own color, in faith, in teaching, and in Her art. Let it not fade in the mission field."[16] This should be applied not only to clear-cut mission fields, of course, but also to Orthodoxy in the diasporas, as today many Orthodox often assimilate aspects of foreign cultures indiscriminately. For, if Father Cosmas' words hold true, then we must not expect the kind of results we see in Kolwezi in our part of the world if we are busy appropriating "the means and methods" of the heterodox. One may have to work very hard to avoid this compromise, yet we have Father Cosmas and the Church in Zaire as testimony that the struggler will have his reward.

---

16 Ibid, p. 41.

Father Cosmas did not stop at simply avoiding the influence of heterodox culture within Zaire. He extended this principle to protect those young souls he sent abroad to study and be formed in the Orthodox way. He writes, "It is almost assured that the young native is destroyed when sent to study in Europe, returning as a theologian only in terms of his degree, not his heart . . . In Kolwezi, we send the pious young man to the monastery of our repentance . . . where he learns the Greek language, theological matters, dogmatics, ethics, worship, the typikon, iconography, and Byzantine music, both in practice and theory. He studies Orthodoxy in the 'university of the desert,' keeping company with sanctified elders and spiritually-gifted fathers and learning from them the 'according to likeness.' Purified, and forming Christ within him, the young candidate becomes a good co-worker and our ideal successor."[17]

Father Cosmas' care for the young native soul sent to study abroad arose out of his deep pastoral sensitivity and not out of any alleged ecclesiastical chauvinism. It was this sensitivity and a blessed single-mindedness and constant focus on bringing his disciples *to the measure of the stature of the fullness of Christ*, and not any misguided idealism, that made it hard for him to countenance disregard of the canons. With respect to the canons governing ordination, this was particularly difficult because suitable candidates were few and the observance of the canons demanded much faith and patience. But, Father Cosmas, together with his Bishop, observed the canons, for they knew that there was a spiritual law at work and a punishment that violators of the canons cannot escape. He writes: "The canons of the Church, of course, must be observed with respect to ordinations. Otherwise, the canons will avenge themselves and we will pay for our concessions (1 Tim. 3: 2-13)." And elsewhere he writes: "In areas where excessive tolerance is shown, the situation continually deteriorates and I am very concerned that at some point it will become incurable."[18]

---

17 Ibid, p. 31.
18 Ibid, p. 32.

Basic Presupposition: Working Under the Local Bishop

Father Cosmas set out from the beginning to carry out a work that was ecclesiastical, without reference to his person but, rather, centered on Christ and His Church. Thus, he came to Africa not as an individual performing a personal undertaking, but as a monk of a specific monastery sent to enlist in the service of the Church under the local Bishop. He would often say, "If my work is my own, it will disintegrate as soon as I leave. If, however, it rests on an ecclesiastical base, the Church will assume it and it will continue."[19]

Father Cosmas wanted everything to be in harmony with the canonical order of the Church. He advanced to the planning and realization of each project he undertook only after securing the blessing of his Bishop. He would not tire of emphasizing "I offer my services with my Metropolitan, His Eminence Timothy Kontomerko."[20]

Even when pressed by his own (according to the flesh) Father's fear that financial support would dry up due to certain problems that had arisen, Father Cosmas remained unwavering in his faithfulness to the ecclesiology of the Church:

"I set out from my monastery with the blessings of my *Geronda* and the other fathers and the explicit command of Father Paisios, who, also, is my spiritual guide, to work together with the heads of the Church for the good of the mission. The Church exists wherever there is a Bishop and faithful flock. Without the Bishop the faithful do not constitute the Church, but a Protestant heresy. Consequently, the line that I follow, working together with the local Bishop, is the most advisable, and yet even if I wanted to do something different, you know that I wouldn't have a blessing from my monastery, anyway."[21]

---

19 *O Ierapostolos*, p. 212.
20 Ibid.
21 See the Letter entitled *Hope Not in Men but in the Lord of the Mission* on page 129.

INTRODUCTION

The shepherd surrounded by his young flock

In cases where the Bishop is a source of problems, Father Cosmas counseled against creating open rifts with him, as they would "harm rather than help." He saw that taking "recourse to a worldly model of contemporary form, . . . toward the finding of justice, produces no results." In such cases, where solutions cannot be found, "then it is preferable that we prudently withdraw with our co-workers, handing over the work to a new contingent, so as not to scandalize innocent souls (Mat. 18:7)."[22]

In response to the opinion of some, that one should not support missionary work in an area where the Bishop is not "beyond reproach," Father Cosmas was not sympathetic. "This position is shown to be baseless and utopian, for, humanly judging the situation, we consider a purification of ecclesiastical leadership as practically impossible and thus we tread from bad to worse, and this in the very age of the Antichrist. All the same, what should be done? Should we stop the evangelization of the nations?

---

22 *Thoughts about Missionary Work from Experience*, p. 8.

Of course not. On the contrary, we will devote ourselves even more to the work of missions and, with the grace of God and our own stability and love, the mission will continue and advance, and the "blameworthy" bishop along with it. The most important point of all, however, is this: we mustn't trust in our own spirituality, sincerity and holiness, if we, in fact, have something of these. 'Let him that thinks he stands take heed lest he fall' (1 Cor. 10:12)."[23]

A Visionary who took One Step at a Time

As a result of conversations with illumined Fathers on Mount Athos and indications he received from his own conscience while on the mission field, Father Cosmas knew that he had to be patient, that the work was just beginning and that he would not see its full flowering in this life. "Continue on," Fr. Paisios told him, "however, the struggle will be a long one, for the people there will be slow in coming to accept Christianity."[24]

With this in mind, then, and being a true Orthodox missionary, Father Cosmas was not anxious or persuaded to adopt short-range solutions. Unlike the missionaries of heterodox groups, Father Cosmas made a point of avoiding a predetermined programmed approach. You won't find references to five-year programs, or slick slogans in the writings of Father Cosmas. He believed that missionary work "is a linkage of one's own temperament, knowledge, possibilities and local conditions. It is not necessary to follow certain molds . . . The missionary is free and when he is open to the grace of God, the Holy Spirit will speak riches in his heart and indicate to him what to do, gradually and in correspondence to the development of the work. Let us leave room for prayer to act

---

23 Ibid, p. 9.
24 See the Letter entitled *The Struggle will be a Long One* on page 131.

New generations, partakers of Father Cosmas' "sweet fruit."

without rushing the situation with narrow logic, absolute measures or the assessments of critics at each stage."[25]

Father Cosmas was a visionary who took one step at a time. He understood early on that he must see things in terms of generations not years. Thus it was that he laid great stress on the upbringing and training of the young men and women under his care, for the future leadership of the Church. It was for this reason that, in addition to the founding of a monastery, he undertook the establishment of boarding houses at the Mission Center, where young men and women came to stay, study, pray, learn and grow into mature Orthodox Christians. Today, twenty-two

---

25 Ibid, p. 18.

Father Cosmas' successor, Father Meletios, speaking to the faithful.

years later, the children that first took up residence at the Mission Center have become the clerical, monastic and lay leaders of the Church in Zaire, just as Father Cosmas foresaw.

A Fruit-bearing Tree for Generations to Come

Father Cosmas was an exemplification of the Gospel saying of the Lord: "Except a grain of wheat fall into the ground and die, it abideth alone: but if it die, it bringeth forth much fruit" (John 12:24). His life was a series of "precious deaths" to the "old man" which made his bodily death "fruit-bearing." These fruits are now offered not just to those who knew him while he lived, but also to all those who have since, and will in the future, come to know Christ and follow Him into the mission field through Father Cosmas' example. "The seed has fallen into the earth," writes Abbot George. "It dies, for if it does not die, it will not sprout forth a beautiful tree, with the sweetest of fruits, under which many souls will find rest."[26]

Already Abbot George's words have found bountiful fulfillment, not just in Kolwezi, but also throughout the Orthodox world. The greatness of Father Cosmas' work and example lies, as he himself has said, in that it has not died with him but continues, on an even greater scale. And not only the work he began in Kolwezi, but also the work of Orthodox mission worldwide. Today, this namesake of Holy Cosmas Aitolos, that regenerator of the race of Hellenes, stands as torchbearer for missionaries to the races of men the world over, in Africa, Latin America and Asia. They cite him as their inspiration and the archetype for their own work.

In Madagascar, in the span of six short years, the Orthodox Church has been established through the grace of God and under the leadership of the missionary-Bishop Nektarios. Since 1994 over 12,000 souls have been baptized, 62 parishes founded and 26 churches built. His Grace Bishop Nektarios had the blessed Father Cosmas as his model. He looked to his example when starting out, in the erecting of churches, in the providing of philanthropy, in the visiting of prisons and hospitals, with the feeding of the hungry and, in general, in the whole work of the mission.

On the other side of the world, in Taiwan, there is another "disciple" of Father Cosmas, the Hieromonk Jonah. He, too, looks up to heaven at the flaming example of Father Cosmas for inspiration and guidance in his newly founded mission. He has only just begun (2001), and the obstacles and challenges facing him are enormous, yet, as with Father Cosmas, his "disposition to self-sacrifice and self-denial," and "aim of leaving his bones among the natives" has already made it possible for God to act mightily.

Who will be the next to follow in Blessed Father Cosmas' footsteps? The Lord alone, Who knows every soul before its coming into the world, speaks and reveals which monk or layman should enter next into His vineyard for the reaping of the harvest. When it came time for Father Cosmas to depart

---

26 Archimandrite George of Grigoriou, *speech given the day after the sudden death of Fr. Cosmas.*

this life, the Lord revealed to him his successor in Kolwezi. His Abbot George tells us that, "shortly before his final departure [from Mount Athos] for Africa and his death, he visited Father Meletios in his cell and told him that he would continue his work."[27] And, indeed, a few months later, days after Father Cosmas departed this life, Abbot George called Father Meletios in to suggest that he succeed Father Cosmas, without, however, knowing anything of what Father Cosmas had predicted.

So, the work of the Church will by no means cease, for He "who desires that all be saved and come to the knowledge of the Truth" is constantly raising up workers for His Vineyard. It is sufficient only that we imitate such blessed ones as Father Cosmas and "hate our life in this world" and "die to it," so as to "keep it for eternity." Then, perhaps, we, too, may be counted worthy of treading that path which guides one on the beautiful journey of our Christian race, which Father Cosmas blazed so resolutely.

Fr. Peter Alban Heers
Feast of Saint Cosmas Aitolos, Equal to the Apostles
August 24, 2001

---

27 Archimandrite George of Grigoriou, *Reflections*, p. 99.

Apostle to Zaire

Father Cosmas, as a layman in Africa, oversaw the rapid
construction of holy churches to the glory of God.
This picture was taken four days into work on this church.

THE LIFE
of Blessed Father Cosmas Grigoriatis

By his father, Demetri Aslanidis

Birth and Upbringing

I, Dimitrios Aslanidis, the writer of this present biography, married Despina Xenidou on 29 June 1941, the day of the Holy Apostles Ss. Peter and Paul, after the Greek-Italian War. We lived in the village of Theodosia, Kilkis. A few months later, Despina became pregnant. At the same time, she started bleeding inexplicably from her nose and mouth, and this continued until she was in her last month. During this month, she had fainting fits as well, two or three times a day. On 16 August, 1942, she gave birth to a handsome baby boy. All the troubles she had came to an end and all the trials were forgotten.

Then began the care of the child. My father, John was his name, whenever he was able to take time off from all the farm work he had to do, would come running and pick the boy up in his embrace. He never wanted to hear him screaming and crying.

My father-in-law was a priest, and before a month had passed he suggested that we baptize the boy. So we brought the font home, the godmother, and our friend and relative, Mrs. Angela Papadopoulou arrived and the Mystery began. I told the godmother to name the boy John, after my father, who was delighted when he heard it and said that we had given the boy that name so that he would look after them in their old age.

Our son John grew up under the German Occupation of Greece. Food was scarce in the marketplaces and people in the cities died of starvation.

Even in the villages, farmers suffered because they were forced to sell their bread to buy other necessities.

There were no special foods for children, such as there are today. The whole family ate the same food. I remember, in the spring of 1942, when we were planting seed potatoes, there were none left over to eat. So I saved 3–4 kilos, put them in a container and told my wife to keep them for the child. Fortunately, we had sheep and cows, so we were able to ensure that the child had food.

Even as a child, John appeared to be an intelligent child. Once, we lost the lid of a teapot we had and not long after went with John to the house of my father-in-law, the priest, on some job or other. The boy, who was no more than a year and a half old, found a similar lid where he was playing and brought it to me, making gestures at the same time. "Take it," I told him. Straight away, he stowed it in his clothes and, when we got home, put it on the teapot all by himself. But there were other events, too, which showed that he was intelligent and lively at games.

Until October 1944, we suffered badly under the Germans. Once they had gone, we rejoiced for a brief period in our freedom, but then the Civil War began. In the meantime, in 1945, my second son, Alexander, was born. Then, for fear of the war, I left my village and spent most of the time in Kilkis or Thessaloniki. The children and their mother remained in the village, afraid. In January 1947, my wife, who was pregnant with the third child, loaded the other two onto a donkey and came to Thessaloniki, fleeing the fire of the rebels. They came without any goods or supplies, with fear in their hearts, scarcely making it.

Three months earlier I had rented a shack from my cousin Constantine. I divided it down the middle with some wickerwork and put some tools in one of the rooms—I worked as an iron dealer—and a single bed in the other. For a good long time, all four of us were obliged to sleep in that single bed. In the meantime, in June 1947, the third child, Stavroula, was born. From January to August 1947 we lived in the shop and then in a cement room until 1952. When we were put out of there, we bought a plot of land and built a shack, where we lived until 1959. Then, by God's grace, we built our own house, where we live to this day.

Studies

In 1948, John started at the Primary School of Stavroupolis. When he finished school for the day, I used to assign him a couple of jobs in the shop and when I was away he would look after it himself. He learned to sell a variety of things and to make a few small objects himself, as far as his strength allowed. As he grew up, he made more difficult tools, which were useful in our line of work, and I often adopted his suggestions.

At school, he quickly earned the love of his teachers, because of his willingness to do any task they assigned him. He learned to change the panes in the school windows and other useful jobs. He was good at his lessons without being distinguished. He had a practical rather than academic brain. He was a lively child, but not to the point of being troublesome. With joy he would haul vegetables for the rabbits we kept in the backyard. When he didn't have work to do, he would go for rides with his sister in a little cart he had.

One day he was disobedient and, because I was strict and used to give them the rod, he was afraid to come home in the evening and slept in the shop on a bench. When I arrived there in the morning, everything was gleaming. In that way he appeased me and got out of being punished.

John knew the market in Thessaloniki from the time he was 10. He did the shopping for anything light enough. If it were heavier, up to 70 kilos, he would load it onto his bike, take a three-wheeled barrow or sometimes a horse and cart and bring it home. In this way, he eased my burden considerably.

He was very daring. When I built the shack in 1952, with corrugated iron on the outside and bricks on the inside, a snake would often come there to drink, because there were fields all round then. One day John saw the snake going into a hole. I was away at the shop. Without any fear, he picked up a hoe, dug out the hole, found the snake and killed it. It was a meter and a half long.

Life in the Church

From when he was a young child, John was never absent from Church. Catechism classes were his meat and drink. And whatever he learned, he would come and tell me, so that I would be happy, too. In 1954, he left Primary School and then enrolled in the Middle Catechism School at "The Lighthouse" of the "Zoë" Brotherhood. Every Sunday morning, he used to get up before me and go to Church down in the city. After that, he would attend catechism lessons and, when he came back at half past one, he would be full of joy and liveliness.

At the age of 14, he enrolled in the Catechism School of the YMCU (The Young Greek Men's Christian Union). He met some good young people there, and became friends with Haralambos Kalaïtzidis, for whom he was later best man and whose first child, Vasiliki, he baptized, and also Demos Tsifoutidis, now abbot of the Monastery of Kostamonitou on Mount Athos, with the name of Archimandrite Agathon. He also got to know and became close to the late abbot of the Monastery of Xeropotamou, Fr. Ephraim of blessed memory. Another friend was Apostolos Stefiadis, from Neapolis, now a Professor of Mathematics, and there were many others.

Apart from their catechism lessons, they would gather in the evenings on feast days, on the roof of our house or somewhere else and read the Holy Scriptures or other Christian books. They also played games they had learned at catechism and at camp. As for the late rector of our parish, Fr. Apostolos, they were his right hand in providing assistance and services.

Technical School and Other Pursuits

When John left Primary School, I wanted to send him to Middle School, but the late priest of our parish, Papa-Michalis, suggested sending him to learn a trade, because he would make more money than better-educated people. I agreed to his suggestion and sent him to work on elevators with a neighbour of ours.

I soon changed my mind, however, and sent him instead to an electrician, so he could go to a technical school. He worked there for a short time, received a certificate and went with his mother to enrol in the "Euclid" school. It was private, because at that time there were still no state schools. As a working electrician, he laboured hard, taking loads of electrical equipment right up Saint Demetrios Street as far as the Acropolis. I comforted him, telling him that better days were on their way. Other children railed at him, but he kept his patience for a year.

Then he found another good person, Loupinis, who has reposed now, and worked for him all day before going on to school in the evening. He would get back home at 11–12 in the evening by bike. Then he used to eat, read, write and go to sleep. Next morning, before we managed to see him he was away.

In 1960, he finished the Lower School of Electrical Mechanics and received his certificate. Then he applied to the School for Foreman Electricians and continued going to night school at "Euclid" for another three years. It was then that he took the decision to remain unmarried. He told me four years later. He came back on leave from the Navy, where he was doing his National Service and told me: "Father, tell Ma not to try and fool all the girls around here because she wants to marry me off. I'm going to remain unmarried and serve in the Mission Abroad."

The first contacts with the Foreign Mission were made at the camp of Saint Silas in Kavala. We wrote to the late missionary, Papa-Chrysostomos Papasarandopoulos, who was then in Kenya and Uganda, in Africa. Thereafter we continued to keep in touch with events through the missionary bulletins and later through a periodical called "On the Way."

Thessaloniki 1959: The future Father Cosmas (second from left) gathers experience for his future as a missionary. He is pictured here with his co-workers at the national electric company.

Because his boss's work dropped off, John found a temporary job with the electric company, working on the overhead wires. This was dangerous, he was exposed to the elements winter and summer, but he enjoyed this risky work. Two years later, he was taken on permanently, but resigned soon afterwards. I asked him: "Why have you resigned, now that you've been taken on permanently?" He answered: "Because it would be unfair to keep the position. It would stop somebody else earning his bread. And I'm bound for another position, a higher one."

Military Service

In 1963, he finished at the "Euclid" School and enrolled at a private night school in Thessaloniki. But he then left immediately to do his national service, without studying there at all. In September 1964, he returned on a short leave, studied the year's work a little and passed the class, without actually attending any lessons. For the second year, he enrolled in a state night school in Piraeus, which was near the Naval base where he was posted. So he managed to be both a sailor and a student. After the Navy, he finished with the Secondary School, since he attended lessons while he was staying as a boarder at the Brotherhood of "The Cross."

To do his national service, he was first sent to the Piraeus naval base. He did his training there and was then posted to the anti-torpedo craft the "Sfendoni" (Sling) as a petty officer, second class. He served on the ship from February 1964 until the December of the same year. The rest of his term he spent on land, at a shore station at Skaramanga. He was discharged in March 1966, having served 30 months.

Because of his faith and love for Christ, he brought charges against officers for blaspheming and had them punished, while if he heard sailors blaspheming, he punished them himself.

The Brotherhood of the Holy Cross and Other Studies

Before leaving for his National Service, he had heard a great deal about Archimandrite Avgoustinos Kantiotis, his sermons and his struggles. When he heard him for the first time, he was so pleased that thereafter he never left him again.

On one of his leaves from the Navy, he revealed his secret to me. Since I knew that from as early as 1965 he had made the decision to become a priest how could I stand in the way of his future? When he realized my heart's desire, which was for him to become a priest, he said: "For the

John (Father Cosmas) is to the right of Fr. Avgoustinos (center) with the members and colleagues of the Brotherhood of the Holy Cross. The mosaic plaque in the foreground reads "struggle."

time being, I'm not ready. I'll remain a few years with Fr. Avgoustinos, to strengthen myself spiritually, because he's the best I've come across in spiritual matters, and then we'll see. Now you tell mother, so that she doesn't cry when I leave you after having finished with the Navy." Indeed, my wife was in agreement and then he said to the other children: "If you can all manage to become monks and nuns, I'll be very happy."

After the Navy, he came home for a couple of days, sorted out some of his affairs, said goodbye to us and went back down to Athens and Fr. Avgoustinos. John had benefited a good deal from his acquaintance with Fr. Avgoustinos' other spiritual children, many of whom are clergymen today. He was a particular favourite of Nikolaos Sotiropoulos, a theologian.

Until 1970, when he finished with the secondary school, he used to come up and see us in Thessaloniki only in the breaks, while later on he was always free. At the beginning he had to do with the basement of the Brotherhood's house, with a maintenance team, but then he worked with great success in the printing shop as head of printing. When those responsible for the Brotherhood saw his capabilities, they assigned building tasks to him.

In 1967, Fr. Avgoustinos became Metropolitan of Florina. John then started going up to Florina regularly to offer his valuable services and technical advice for the construction of churches, institutions, Gypsy settlements and a whole host of Crosses. He had put together a team of experienced technicians and with the young men of the brotherhood's house, whom he roped in as volunteers, he ran all over the place on various jobs for the Metropolis.

Among the largest tasks were the Gypsy Settlement, the Old People's Home, the Brotherhood's house and three large Crosses. One was put up in the village of Sitaria, on the church of Saint Cosmas, another on the lake of Little Prespa, and the third on hill 802, near the town of Florina.

The last of these was 32 meters high and 14 wide. It needed a lot of effort to build, according to what John told me later. The Army, in fact, made its mules available to bring up the building materials. When the builders got to the crossroads with the horizontal arms, they threw up their hands in despair, saying to John that it was impossible to fix a wooden mould onto the vertical stem. And they were quite right, when you think that each arm was 7 meters long. John was not downcast, however, nor would he give up the job in hand. He undertook to fix it himself. He hung in the air by one hand and with the other nailed planks together at a height of 28 meters. When the Metropolitan learned of it he was amazed and could hardly believe it.

It was from then that his right arm began to hurt. It had already been painful, in fact, from 1967, though he had not stopped working, but had merely avoided heavy duty.

In his personal diary he wrote: "I talked with five doctors for an hour and the outcome was that my arm was not going to get any better and would in their opinion remain paralyzed. The whole business started

For nine years, as a member of the Holy Cross Brotherhood, Father Cosmas served the work of Internal Mission.

in the basements in the Diocese of Florina, as I was cutting the metal bands round packages. I don't believe it's from sin, because I got what I'm suffering from through excessive zeal for the Mission, as God is my witness."

Among his private papers I found an envelope full of X-rays of his arm. He told me that at the Red Cross and Annunciation Clinics, the doctors had recommended cutting it off, because it would only be a nuisance for the rest of his life. But God proved them wrong.

Apart from the Diocese of Florina, he also worked with his team on Paros, on a building in the birthplace of Fr. Avgoustinos, which was used as a library. Whenever he had any time, he would go to the Monastery of Longovarda and drink from the flowing stream of the spiritual teaching of the great Elder and Abbot, Fr. Philotheos Zervakos.

All the time he was in Athens working and boarding at the Brotherhood of the Cross, he also learned other trades. He went to the Red Cross for a year to learn nursing, so that he could use his knowledge

The Brotherhood of the Holy Cross

Fr. Cosmas in the garden of the Rizareio Ecclesiastical Academy.

later in the Foreign Mission. At the same time he attended lessons on the Foreign Mission at *Apostoliki Diakonia* given by Professor Elias Voulgarakis and the Bishop of Androusa, Anastasios Yannoulato. He also attended Catechism lessons at the Archdiocese of Athens, where he worked for 12 years as a teacher in various parishes.

One of his pupils, Apostolos Diaremes, followed him to the Foreign Mission. Papa-Cosmas first took him to the Monastery of Gregoriou, where he would later become a monk. The young man was tonsured, given the new name Kyrillos and then taken by Papa-Cosmas to the Mission. Today Fr. Kyrillos works tirelessly, following in the footsteps of his teacher and Elder.

John even went so far as to become proficient in swimming, gaining a special certificate. He loved the sea and provided himself with all the necessary lifesaving equipment. When he went to the monastery he left it all behind at home, but he did need the technique later in the Mission. He dived about twenty meters and pulled out a child who had drowned and lay in the mud at the bottom of an artificial lake at Kolwezi.

He did not even hesitate to offer his blood to those in need. He had a rare blood group and when he heard or read in the news bulletins that blood of this type was needed, he would hurry off and give it. He told me once that he had heard on the radio, after midnight, that his blood group was needed to save some patient. He set off quickly and gave it.

After ten years with Fr. Avgoustinos, he remembered the Foreign Mission again and wanted to take lessons on other subjects, so that he would be better qualified to meet the needs and difficulties of the task ahead. He took entrance exams for medicine because he wanted to help the foreign mission as a doctor. At the same time he also took exams for the Rizareio Ecclesiastical Academy, at the uppermost level. He failed to get into the medical faculty but passed the exams for the Ecclesiastical Academy. He then left Fr. Avgoustinos and studied for a year without a break.

In 1975, he continued with the second year of his studies. He was by nature very lively and a strong defender of his positions in spiritual matters and affairs. He told me that he often fell out with his teachers on a variety of subjects. Through the school, he formed a circle of students with whom he read books beneficial to the soul and whom he helped with their spiritual development, since he was older and had a great deal of experience in many areas.

After he had concluded his studies there, I suggested that he go to the Theological Faculty, but he said it was not necessary, since the teachers at the Rizareio Academy had been essentially university-level professors. In any case, the time had come for him to work for the Mission Abroad. So that was the last stage in his formal education, the Rizareio Ecclesiastical Academy. Altogether, he studied for 24 years, i.e.:

6 at Public School
7 at evening classes
4 at the Lower School of Electrical Technicians
3 at the Foremen's School
2 at the Higher Ecclesiastical Academy

1 at the Nurse's School of the Red Cross and
1 at the Catechism School of *Apostoliki Diakonia*

All of this learning and his practical experience were of considerable help in the foundation of the Missionary Unit and at the beginning of his spiritual and missionary work in the town of Kolwezi, in Zaire.

The Republic of Zaire

Father Cosmas, a layman, stands next to Archimandrite Amphilochios (center) and his co-worker, Father Seraphim.

The First Period of the Mission

As we said, after the first year of his studies at the Rizareio Ecclesiastical Academy, he went down to Africa for a year. He took this decision when he met the missionary Amfilohios Tsoukos in Athens and was told of the great needs of the Mission. He telephoned us to tell us he would be going to be with Fr. Amfilohios. He came to Thessaloniki, packed his bags and went back down to Athens to depart.

In July 1975, John was in Kolwezi, Zaire. It was here that his great struggles began. Fr. Amfilohios set him the task of constructing churches in towns and villages which were within a radius of 700 kilometers. With the enthusiasm, dynamism and daring for which he was outstanding,

The First Period of the Mission

Father Cosmas with his fellow laborers and builders.
They built 9 churches in the short span of 15 months.

he began the work immediately, entirely unhindered by the unknown language, Swahili, which he now heard for the first time.

He set up work teams and began to work on the foundations of churches. The teams worked one after another. In other words, one of them did the building, then came the plasterers, others put in the doors and windows, others again did the painting and so on. Before one church was finished, another would be started. He had to finish what Fr. Amfilohios had set him to do.

The news we had from the nuns Anastasia and Zoë and especially from Fr. Amfilohios was very pleasant and encouraging. John was matchless and untiring in his work and scorned all danger to his life.

All this church building required a great deal of money. The nuns of the Mission wrote letters here, there and everywhere, asking for help. And, indeed, the money came in and building work on the churches

Father Cosmas, as a lay *ierapostolos*, pauses
for a picture with his young spiritual brothers.

continued. In 15 months, John built 9 churches. Of these, 8 were in the Samba region and one in Kananga, in the missionary region of Archimandrite Hariton Pnevmatikakis.

At that time, Mr. Simos, the Chairman of the Patras Missionary Association, "The First-Called" was there on a visit. He told us on his return that John would lie down on his bed to rest with his shoes on. He did not want to waste any time on himself.

In the meantime, in Kolwezi, the Metropolitan of Central Africa, the late Kyros Nicodemos Galatsiatos, was so taken with him that he honoured him with the gold medal of the Patriarchate of Alexandria.

Because he took no care for himself, since he was so strongly built, he fell ill with sunstroke. For the rest of his life he suffered from headaches and dizziness. Despite his tiredness and his many concerns, he never failed to keep in touch with us by letter. He believed that others would be found to follow in his footsteps. Many young people wrote to him that they were considering the Mission, but later they married. Others were ordained priests in Greece and, once they had been allotted a position in a parish and were set up, forgot their promises. Yet other people, on whom he had never set any hopes, went and helped him, and this is still the case today.

Return to Greece

In September 1976, he returned from Zaire and continued his studies in the second year of the Rizareio Ecclesiastical Academy. The following year he got his certificate and went with Fr. Nicodemos Bilalis to the Holy Mountain. Fr. Nicodemos had collected money for the reconstruction of the church of Saint Nicodemos the Athonite, near the *kelli* where the saint lived and fell asleep in the Lord. He found John to be the right man to undertake the rebuilding and assigned him the task. And indeed, through the dynamism that was so characteristic of him, he had the skeleton of the church up in three months, in the summer of 1977. It needed a great deal of work because the ground was uneven and sloping.

At this time, John found the opportunity to visit virtuous Athonite fathers, too. Among them was Fr. Paisios, who was then living on land belonging to the Monastery of Stavronikita, at Kapsala. He suggested that John should be tonsured a monk at the Holy Monastery of Gregoriou, with which until then he had no contact or acquaintance; that he should be ordained and then go back to the Mission as a hieromonk, with the blessing of his monastery.

John told me of his first meeting and introduction to Fr. Paisios. After he had introduced himself, the Elder, without any other answer, sent him off with a jug to fetch water from a spring, which was some distance from the *kelli*. John took the jug and went off willingly, found the faucet, which ran in a fine trickle and, after waiting patiently for long enough, made his way back. The Elder took the jug and emptied it in front of him into the cistern of the *kelli*. He had wanted to test the patience

St. Paisios of Mount Athos (+1994)

and obedience of John. They spoke at length at that time and John was greatly benefited by the divinely illumined counsels of the Elder.

Another time, he told me, before he went to the Monastery of Gregoriou, he again visited Fr. Paisios. On the way, it rained so heavily that he was dripping wet. As he approached the outer gate of the Elder's kelli, he found him outside with some old clothes, waiting for his visitor. John was at a loss to understand how the Elder knew that anyone was coming to his *kelli*. They went inside. The Elder wanted to give him another pair of trousers to change into but he only had the one! So he lit the stove for him. John warmed himself and dried off. They talked for a long time and John realized what a great gift it is from God to have the advice of one of the enlightened Elders of the desert.

At the Holy Monastery of Gregoriou

At that time, Fr. Nicodemos Bilalis was living at New Skete, which belongs to the Monastery of Ayiou Pavlou. John paid him a visit. He also wanted to see the spiritual father of the skete, Fr. Spyridon Xenon, who was living with a brotherhood of 4 other monks in the skete. Fr. Spyridon undertook to introduce John to the Abbot of the Monastery of Gregoriou, Fr. George, as a prospective monk.

So they went together to the monastery, one morning in October 1977. The regulations of the monastery, and of the Holy Mountain as a whole, make no provision for missionary expeditions on the part of new monks, for obvious reasons. In the case of John, the Abbot exercised *oikonomia*, submitting both to Fr. Spyridon and the venerable Elder Paisios, who also suggested that John be tonsured at Grigoriou before going to the Mission soon afterwards. The fathers of the Monastery agreed with the Abbot, Fr. George.

With the consent of the Monastery, John went out into the world again for a short time. He put his affairs and obligations in order. He went to see his spiritual father, Fr. Photios Stamatopoulos, as well as the former Archbishop of Thessaloniki, Leonidas Paraskevopoulos, the Metropolitan of Florina, Avgoustinos Kantiotis and other well-known clergymen and friends.

In fact, we went together to see the Metropolitan of Florina. When John told him what he had in mind, Metropolitan Avgoustinos raised certain objections. He did not want to let him go and said: "I want you with me. I've got a great task ahead of me and I need people to help." "I made this decision as long ago as 1960", replied John, "and I have to see it through." When the discussion ended, Metropolitan Avgoustinos turned to me and said, "I want John with me and my wings are broad enough to cover him."

He went into the Monastery in March, 1978. His new Elder, Fr. George, advised him not to concern himself too much with manual work, so

The ordination of Father Cosmas to the Deaconate at the Holy Monastery of Grigoriou, Mount Athos.

that he would have time for his spiritual duties and to learn the working order of the Monastery. From the hieromonks he learned the duties of a priest, from the Typikaris the order of services and so on. He wanted to apply the Athonite monastic rule to the work of the Mission and to teach the Africans the prayer of the heart, from the books and the little experience he would gain from his eight-month stay in the monastery of his repentance.

In June, he was tonsured a monk, taking the name of Saint Cosmas Aitolos. His Elder, Fr. George, told us later that he had decided to give him the name "Methodios", in honour of Saint Methodios of Thessaloniki, the Enlightener of the Slavs, but he was unable to find a Dismissal Hymn for this saint in the Church prayer-book. Since the moment of his tonsure was approaching, the Elder, by divine indication, named him Monk Cosmas, to honour the great Missionary of Greece during the time of enslavement to the Turks. John, or Father Cosmas as he now was, told his Elder that it was divine enlightenment which had caused him to give him that particular name, because he had always had Saint Cosmas as a protector in his life and had his icon above his pillow, as he later showed him.

He then wrote us a letter about his tonsure and we wished him all the best. He also told us about the great event of his ordination, which was to take place on 15 August (Old Style), in the year 1978. He also wrote to his spiritual father, Fr. Photios, who was in Athens, to get his spiritual consent. He sent this, but was unable to be present in person because of his great age. Those of us in Thessaloniki filled a whole bus and arrived at Ouranoupolis on the eve of the feast of the Mother of God. Others had arrived from all over Greece, especially from Athens and Patras. We were about a hundred men in all and travelled to the Monastery on a boat, which we chartered. It was the first time the fathers of the Monastery had seen so many people for the ordination of one of their brothers.

The ordination to the diaconate took place during the Divine Liturgy of the Feast, which fell on a Saturday, and the next day he was ordained priest. The Abbot, Fr. George, spoke in the refectory, referring to the life and conduct of Fr. Cosmas and thanking, on his behalf, all those who shared in the joy of his ordination. Thereafter, the Bishop of Rodostolos, who conducted the ordination to the diaconate, spoke and after him the Bishop of Androusa, who described Fr. Cosmas' decision as a great and good work of God.

In accordance with the *typicon* of our Church, Fr. Cosmas stayed in the Monastery 40 days, to celebrate 40 liturgies. Then he left the Mountain and prepared his papers for departure, going down to Athens, as well.

He then returned to the monastery of his confession for a few days. He said that before he left, his Elder read a special prayer and expressed the wish that God would further his work. All the fathers of the Monastery, in order of seniority, then bade him farewell, some unable to hold back their tears. He stayed at our house for only two days and then went down to Athens with his things for the great journey.

With the white-haired elder-missionary, Father Hariton.

The Second Mission Period

The first time he went to Zaire and saw, in Kananga, that Fr. Hariton Pnevmatikakis and Sister Olga were old and alone, he thought it would be a good idea to go and be with them. In Athens, however, he met the Metropolitan of Central Africa, Timotheos, and received other instructions. His Grace suggested that he go to the Kolwezi Mission Headquarters, since Fr. Amfilohios had left for Greece and they were in need of a priest. But Fr. Cosmas preferred to make a start from Kananga. He was welcomed with great joy by Fr. Hariton and Sister Olga.

He soon realized that he would not be able to implement there the programme he had worked out during his first period in the mission. He saw that the Protestants and Roman Catholics had had their missionaries there for a hundred years and he wanted to help the Africans, too, spiritually as well as materially. His plan was to find a farm to cultivate and also some stockbreeding facilities because material needs certainly had to be met alongside the spiritual ones. So after a month, Fr. Cosmas left for Kolwezi, in obedience to his bishop, because that was the will of God. Kananga lies 1,500 kilometers away from Kolwezi. He took the train and arrived at his destination seven days later, because the trains then did not travel fast but went at the speed of carts. At Kolwezi, he found the two Sisters, Anastasia Pexou and Zoë Mihalaki, who were very pleased to see him. The bishop was especially pleased when he received a letter from Fr. Cosmas from Kolwezi.

He began to put his plan into operation from the very first days. He wanted to build a mission house that would form the first nucleus for the spiritual development of the little children. He built rooms for the children next to the Mission building. He built a stable for animals, as well, and bought a few goats and hens.

Because of the departure from Kinshasa for Greece of Fr. Dionysios Beka, who worked for the mission, Fr. Cosmas went there for two months, on the instructions of the bishop. He also took a young African with him who knew French and was able to complete many jobs for him. The most important thing was that he was able to claim the ownership of a plot of land which the authorities had handed over for an Orthodox church and which they were anxious to take back. He went to see ministers and other state officials and was able to have the claim officially recognized.

He also managed to find ways of getting tractors and cars tax-free. He was helped from Greece by his friend Michael Hatziioannou and the Missions Abroad Brotherhood of Thessaloniki, which sent him 1,000,000 *drachmas* in 1978 to buy a car.

When he returned from Kinshasa, his goats and hens were nowhere to be found. Thieves had stolen them in the night, having first locked the door of the children's boarding house from the outside. It was this that made Fr. Cosmas take a number of measures. He closed off the yard wall, brought in dogs and posted a guard on the door day and night. From then on there were no serious thefts at the Mission building.

The geographical area covered by the Kolwezi Mission extends 70 kilometers towards Zambia, 350 towards Angola, 300 from the town of Lubumbashi and 700 kilometers to the north. In this vast tract of land, with its scattered native villages, all the roads were dirt-tracks, except one which went to Lubumbashi. During the rains, these roads became impassable. This is why Fr. Cosmas wanted new vehicles: so that he could get about without them breaking down or getting stuck in the mud half-way through the journey.

At the time when I was lending a hand at headquarters, we had two old trucks, which broke down on the road two or three times. But Fr. Cosmas had always brought all the tools and the necessary spare parts with him and repaired them.

Once we went together to a village called Moshima, on the way to Zambia. Towards sunset we were going through the forest and we came across a large truck belonging to the G.K.M. Co., full of women and children on their way to Kolwezi. It had been stuck there for two days. Fr. Cosmas pulled up to help, as usual. I told him we should be getting on because night was falling and we did not know what might happen to us in the forest at that time. He took no notice. Picking up his repair tools, he got underneath the truck and quickly found the problem: the pipes carrying the petrol were blocked. Once he had cleaned them, he shouted to the driver: "Take it away!" And off they went, happy as anything and clapping.

Fr. Cosmas took no thought for any danger to his life and used to say to me: "God made me a missionary in this region. Wherever I go, I'll help whoever I come across who has need of me."

The Spiritual Education of the Africans

Apart from his tireless efforts to create the necessary pre-conditions for the support of the members of the headquarters, the children and many Christians, Fr. Cosmas also set great store by the spiritual side of things.

He began with catechism of the Orthodox Christians in teams or groups. Catechism was different for men, for women, for girls and for boys. He put things in their proper order for the Orthodox in Kolwezi.

But what was to become of the Orthodox in other towns and villages a long way off? He must take care to visit them as well. He got a strong vehicle, like a Land Rover, and went round the villages in that, taking with him his personal tent and provisions. He would gather the people of the villages together and speak to them for hours. Using the vehicle battery, he would show them slides of the Holy Mountain, the Holy Land and the religious life of people in Greece, until late into the night. They would light fires to see by and to keep warm. He prepared them for the Divine Liturgy and Holy Communion and in the morning would celebrate the liturgy in huts made of grass and mud. He would then distribute clothing, medical supplies and, sometimes, provisions.

He persuaded those who agreed to embrace Orthodoxy to lay aside their magic-making equipment and believe only in the true God, Jesus Christ. From every village he would take one or two men, the best there were, and keep them at the Mission Center for training for two or three months. He would then send them back to their villages, and later bring them to Mission Base to refresh what he had taught them, because they easily forgot.

He was often forced to stay in their huts, but could never get to sleep for the smell, the insects, the mice, the snakes and all the night-time animals and vermin. But none of this dented his determination, and his one thought was how to help the Africans out of their poverty and misery.

At various conferences organized by the state, to which he was invited by government officials, he told them not to oppress the people, and not to allow their soldiers to rob the villagers, who were often forced to hide in the woods. Because they respected him and valued his opinion, they followed his advice. Nowadays the military are off the streets and people move freely on the city streets.

When Fr. Cosmas went to Kolwezi in 1978, there was only one African priest, Fr. Gerasimos. He had been ordained in 1975 and went running

Mass Baptisms performed by Father Cosmas and other priests.

round all the village parishes on his own. The spiritual work was done with the local catechism teachers, whom Fr. Cosmas regularly taught. They brought their lists of catechumens and candidates for Baptism.

When, in the summer, the rains stopped, he went round the villages with Fr. Gerasimos and baptized the catechumens in the rivers there. A mass Baptism, whether for a few people or many, took two days.

On the first day, those catechumens who were to be baptized were chosen and their family affairs sorted out. This was a major problem for those who had two or three wives. Before being baptized, they would have to choose which of their wives they wanted for a spouse and then marry them. They were also obliged to hand over all their magic-making equipment, because otherwise the devil would trouble them even after their Baptism.

On the second day, there was Matins and the Divine Liturgy, at which only those who were baptized took Communion. Then they all went to the river, where there was the mass confession of faith, the espousal of Christ and rejection of Satan. They all went into the water and the priest baptized them one by one in the name of the Holy Trinity. Thereafter the newly baptized Christians went to church and partook of the Spotless Mysteries, since the priest had not yet consumed all the Body and Blood. Then the newly baptized couples were married and gifts, clothes and medicines were distributed.

When there were a lot of people to baptize and night fell, the Mysteries were held under the headlights of the vehicle. It was easier to hold Baptisms in cities, in cruciform baptisteries, since there was electricity available, which also helped with the other services.

Before Fr. Cosmas went there, there were a good number of believers in the villages, but no priest. At most, a priest visited them once a year, for confession and communion. Fr. Cosmas had to train candidates for the priesthood and the first to take on this high office were his catechism teachers.

In the summer of 1979, His Grace went to Kolwezi. He and Fr. Cosmas visited the villages and ordained 10 of the best of these teachers. Thus the Missionary staff increased to 11 priests, including Fr. Gerasimos, all of whom attended a liturgical seminar that summer and then dispersed to their villages. Most of them took on two or three parishes each. Every summer they went for two months to Missionary Base and attended a seminar for priests and catechists.

Fr. Cosmas noted in his diary at that time that these priests were not very well equipped and that better-qualified priests would have to be found from among the children of his mission house. Bishop Timotheos later ordained a further three priests, three deacons and three sub-deacons.

Father Cosmas' chosen and faithful co-workers.

The Farm and Stock-Raising Facilities

In the Zaire region, Greeks, and Europeans in general, had long since established farms with domestic animals. At a distance of 7 kilometers from Kolwezi there was one such farm, belonging to two Greeks, Michael Psathas and George Hadjiharalambos. In 1975, however, the government of Zaire appropriated the white people's properties and gave them to the Africans. Within two years they had nothing left and were then reduced to starvation. Because of this, in 1978, the State once again invited the whites to retake their fields and buildings, although they were in a wretched condition.

The two Greeks mentioned above also regained their farm, from which not only were the animals missing, but also the corrugated iron from the roofs of the buildings. They covered some of the buildings for

The Farm and Stock-Raising Facilities

the animals, but were afraid to stock them, in case the animals were stolen again. They heard that Fr. Cosmas wanted to start a farm and they suggested he buy theirs. An agreement was reached and he took it over in 1979. He initially bought some pigs, five goats, the same number of sheep, three rabbits and a few hens.

The water was a long way from the buildings. They had formerly bought it up to the buildings where the animals were kept by little motors, but these broke down because the water was quite murky. Fr. Cosmas reasoned that it was impossible to fetch water by animal or vehicle over such a long distance. He discovered that from a certain higher point of a neighbouring stream the water could flow down naturally. He decided to bring the water to the animals' pound through a channel. He engaged workers and they set about digging the ditch. It was exhausting work, because in some places the ditch had to be five meters deep, but in autumn 1980, it was finished. The workers were able to relax and the animals had their fill of water.

The great joy that they all felt, however, was succeeded by consternation. In the winter, a lot of rain falls there and the ground breaks up. So the ditch suffered great damage and the water leaked away and did not reach the animals. In 1981, a new project began. The G.K.M. Co. sent two bulldozers and two graders to fix the roads. Fr. Cosmas got permission from the boss of the company and used the machines to construct a road three kilometers long beside the ditch. This road was of great help to the workers, because previously they had been walking over rough country through grass three meters high. They also brought sand, stones and cement in headquarters' vehicles and refinished those parts of the ditch that needed it with cement. At the stream from which the water came he built a strong, double stone wall for a dam and so collected all the water of the river. Today there is no lack of water for the stockbreeding installations. A special channel takes it all round the animal buildings and the water comes out at the bottom. The vegetable gardens are also watered continuously from the same source. The stalls are washed out wonderfully and the water brings the manure to a special place, for the gardens.

In 1981, the animals began to multiply, but the stalls and hen houses were still in a dreadful condition. The pigs bore their litters in the mud, the chickens were dying because rainwater was getting in and, in general, better facilities were needed.

Then Mr. Papadimitrakopoulos, who was in charge of missions in Thessaloniki, sent Fr. Cosmas some useful books on animal husbandry. He read them and produced his own plans for the facilities in the buildings. He made sloping floors of cement for the stalls of the animals, so that they could be washed out easily. He whitewashed the walls to kill the bacteria and other parasites, put new corrugated iron on the roofs and made new, improved feed-boxes for the animals. From then on the animals were able to eat their feed more easily, without either wasting it or trampling on it. He put heating into the hen houses for the winter, so that they wouldn't die of cold. He fixed special large barrels to the wall with their mouths facing outwards. Then he burned wood in them and the heat spread through the hen house, while the smoke came out of the mouths of the barrels. He put the rabbits into special wire hutches so that they would not die of various sicknesses when they bore litters. Today, that farm has attracted the admiration not only of the natives, but also of foreigners and tourists who go to Kolwezi from all over the globe. You can hear them saying: "Ortodox, Ortodox."

The Mission Churches in the Kolwezi Region

Apart from the 10 churches, which Fr. Cosmas built in his first missionary period as a layman in "76, he built another five. There are also three that belong to the Greek communities in three large towns. In Lubumbashi there is the church of the Annunciation of the Mother of God, in Kolwezi, the church of St. George and in Likashi that of the Three Hierarchs. All three are very beautiful. In Lubumbashi, Fr. Cosmas also built another church dedicated to the Holy Proto-Martyr Stephen. It was initially small, but he later bought the plot of land in front and extended the narthex. He also built a baptistery next to the church.

In the village of Karkazembe, which lies just off the main road between the towns of Kolwezi and Lubumbashi, he built the church of the Apostle Thomas. It is bigger than the others and beautiful, with an office, a store-room and a bedroom. In the town of Lubumbashi, in 1987, he built the church of the Nativity of Christ on a 12-acre plot. Next to it were constructed other necessary buildings such as an office, storeroom and rectory, all with electricity and water.

In 1987, three more new churches were built. One was in Likashi, dedicated to St. John the Baptist, with a belfry, office, storeroom, rectory and large courtyard. Sister Stavritsa Zahariou oversaw the construction. The second, in the village of Tsomutente was dedicated to Saint Demetrios and funded by an Athenian, while the third, in the village of Mousounoi, was dedicated to the Ss. Theodore. It is on a large plot of land, has a rectory and was paid for by two sisters from Athens.

In the autumn of 1984, Fr. Cosmas was in Greece. On his return, he stayed in Kinshasa for two months. In that time, he built the church of Saint Mark the Evangelist with money from the Greeks of Kinshasa. Next to it, he built an office with two rooms for the priest to live in. All the Greeks and Africans were grateful, because in the space of two months such a fine, beautiful church had sprung up. The Greeks gave him two cars for the work and for transport, one to bring in equipment and the other for his personal use.

Journeys in Greece

In June 1981, Metropolitan Timotheos called him to Greece, where he himself was staying, for a conference of Missionaries. He came and stayed in Athens for a few days to sort out some affairs relating to the Mission, mainly to do with purchases. Then he came home to us for a few days, before leaving for the monastery of his repentance on the Holy Mountain. He was very tired, in body and spirit, and wanted to find a little peace to pray and reflect. At the Monastery, perhaps because of the change of climate, he fell ill. And besides, another great worry befell him. Somebody told lies about Fr. Cosmas to the priests of the Mission, and they libelled him. This wounded him greatly and it prolonged the length of time he stayed ill in bed.

But in this time of bitterness and sorrow, something happened to bring him joy. One of the young men he had once taught in Athens, Apostolos Diaremes, came to the Monastery with the fixed intention of following Fr. Cosmas to the Mission and staying for good. Fr. Cosmas agreed and took him with him to Africa. Today, Apostolos is a monk, one of the monks of the brotherhood of the Monastery of Grigoriou and, together with Fr. Cosmas' successor, Fr. Meletios, bears the whole burden of the Mission in Kolwezi.

About the middle of November of the same year, he made his preparations to return to the Mission Base. He bought about eight tons of goods, things that were non-existent or difficult to find there, and loaded them onto a ship bound for Zaire. On his return to Kolwezi, the Africans were overjoyed to see him again. He forgave all the priests, and from then on never held the slightest thing against anybody. The metropolitan had already sorted out the business of the libel.

In 1982, he came to Greece for a few days to deal with a personal problem and then went back.

In 1984, he came in June for a missionary conference. He set out his views there and also his complaint against the Mission Office of *Apostoliki Diakonia*, which gave more help to one mission and less to the others. Then he went to the Monastery and rested until November. In December he made the return journey with Fr. Kyrillos, who had been in the Monastery for more than a year as a novice and was now a *rasophoros* monk.

His last journey was in June 1988. He stayed in Athens for a week. He saw some friends and colleagues and bought some things, which he sent to Kolwezi. He stayed in Thessaloniki for about ten days. He visited

Fr. Kyrillos oversees the farming operation.

friends of the mission within Thessaloniki and outside and also went up to Siderokastro. There he met Sister Paraskevi Saha, who was living as a novice in a convent. Having been to Kolwezi in 1985, she decided to work permanently on Fr. Cosmas' Mission staff as nurse and person responsible for the girls in the mission house and for the women workers. Later, when she donned the monastic habit, she took the name Xeni.

Fr. Cosmas stayed in the monastery of his repentance for about two months. With the aid of the fathers of the monastery he wrote his Mission Diary, as well as a work on ways of aiding and promoting the missionary task. This was published in the periodical "Foreign Mission" in Thessaloniki, under the title: "Thoughts on Missionary Work from Experience." He received further training in the liturgical rule, celebrated the Divine Liturgy often and, in general, assisted in the difficult tasks of the Monastery.

Towards the end of August, he went out into the world again. He began to give talks all over Greece to help spread the Mission. In Thessaloniki, he was in constant contact with the head of the Mission, who was very fond of him, helped him financially and, like a father, urged him to be more sparing of his strength. But Fr. Cosmas gave no thought whatsoever to himself. He even travelled at night so as to move his work forward. Perhaps he had foreknowledge that his years on this earth would be few.

In Athens, he met a great many people connected with the Mission and spoke to them about the Mission Abroad. At the beginning of October, he went to Cyprus at the invitation of friends of the Mission there. He got to know many people who helped him financially, talked with them and was given a great deal of moral and material support.

When Fr. Cosmas returned from Cyprus with Sister Xeni, they made ready to leave on October 14, 1988. I was rather upset about this and said to George, my fourth child, when I spoke to him on the telephone on the evening of October 12: "What, he isn't going to come and see us? How does he know if he'll ever see us again?" I was thinking of my own death, or that of my wife, but the opposite happened. Fr. Cosmas obeyed. The next evening he came to Thessaloniki by the nine o'clock flight and came straight home. We saw him for a short time and in the morning, at 5 o'clock, he again left for Athens and thence, at noon, for Zaire.

The Mission Staff at Kolwezi

The first labourer for the evangelization of the natives of the Kolwezi region was the late Fr. Chrysostomos Papasarandopoulos, a well-known personality. He worked in Africa for about 12 years. It was there that he left his body, having suffered much and having baptized the first Orthodox Christians in Kolwezi.

In 1973, Fr. Amfilohios Tsoukos went with Sisters Anastasia and Zoë.

Later, Fr. Seraphim Parharidis arrived from Rhodes. Fr. Amfilohios stayed in Kolwezi until 1977, but the sisters stayed on until '79 and worked with Fr. Cosmas for seven months.

In '79, Maria Argyropoulou went there from Thessaloniki and stayed until July '80, when she returned.

In 1981, I went with Kostas Filippou. He stayed for two months, while I was there till March '82.

In 1981, Apostolos Diaremes went, and remained permanently on the staff.

In 1982, Thanos Tzotzos, a dentist from Argos, went there for six months, as did a nurse called Eleni.

In 1983, I went there again and stayed till March '85.

In 1984, the sailor Vasilis Ververis, from Volos, went there for 10 months.

In 1985, Sister Paraskevi Saha, a nurse, went there and stayed on a permanent basis. She is the nun, Xeni, mentioned earlier.

In 1985, I went for a third time and stayed 11 months, returning because of my wife's ill health.

In 1987, Theano Mousdekelidou went for three months.

In 1987, V. Ververis went for a further 6 months and in 1988 Thanos Tzotzos returned for 6 more months. All of these were good colleagues of Fr. Cosmas, and continue to offer their services to this day to his successor, Fr. Meletios.

How the Mission Worked

When certain people in Greece discovered that Fr. Cosmas had started a farm in Africa without their knowledge, they mistrusted his motives and put it about that he had gone there to set himself up for life. They were unaware of his plans and of his thinking and this is why they were slow to provide him with financial assistance, as they did other Mission Headquarters. Either that or they sent him only very little. Fr. Cosmas, of course, was

Great lengths: the transportation of water for the building of churches some thirty kilometers away (1976).

not downhearted, but worked all the harder, in order to prove to everyone that his intentions were pure and that he loved the Mission and the Church. By night he would study his plans and by day he put them into operation.

He was very careful with his expenses and never wasted money. He always used to find ways of getting materials as cheaply as possible. For example, he fixed up five brick-making machines, which baked the bricks with wood, without spending a penny, because he found useless bits of iron on abandoned farms in the forest and made good use of them. Instead of buying stones, he used workers to get them from a particular area where wages were low and so it worked out better. Later still, the G.K.M Co. gave him the stones free. If he had bought the bricks, it would have cost him, but as it was, he had them for next to nothing. He also had his workers bring sand from a place where there was plenty. He bought good sand only for the cement. He never bought cement from merchants, but direct from the factory, either with a 40-ton train wagon or a lorry with 800 bags delivered to the Mission Base. Apart from that, transport was very expensive there, so he was obliged to buy his own trucks to transport material.

A great deal of wood was also required for a variety of tasks: the children's kitchen at the mission house, the heating for the poultry, the food for the pigs and for baking bricks. Altogether, a truckload of wood was required every day, which would have cost a great deal. So Fr. Cosmas went to the state authorities and asked them to let him have a part of the forest for woodcutting, free, for the needs of the Orthodox Mission. The request was granted. The wood was cut by workers, stacked and then loaded onto the mission truck.

For the construction work, the plastering, the painting, the wiring and so on, Fr. Cosmas set up special teams, which worked under his supervision. When the team began work, he would keep an eye on the builders, the plasterers and so on. And so the churches went up at a great rate. He used, formerly, to buy the beams for the roofs, but then later they cut down tall eucalyptus trees which were on the land given to the Mission by the government. He took chain saws to them and so they had their beams ready made.

Animal feed is extremely expensive in those countries, because it is all imported from abroad. This was why almost all the farms folded. Fr. Cosmas found a way to make the fewest possible purchases here, too. For the hens that were laying, he bought food. Why? Because an egg cost half a day's wages there. Rabbit food was cheap, while it simply was not worth buying food for the pigs. All the white people who had pigs on their farms abandoned them, because it was not worth buying them food. The good Lord enlightened Fr. Cosmas, however, and, after much experiment, he got them their food for next to nothing. This was the trunk of the banana tree, which the pigs ate a lot of. The banana tree trunks are cut up small and boiled with the husks of the barley, which the factories use to make beer in those parts. A very good and nutritious food results, to which a little corn can be added from time to time to help fatten the pigs.

Through these animals, almost half the expenses of the mission were met. The children of the mission house ate the meat, while whole pigs were often given to the prisoners, the lepers and hospitalized patients, for whom no food was provided by the state, other than what their relatives brought. There were about 500 pigs, 300–500 rabbits and up to 3,000 hens. There were also other fowl, such as ducks, guinea hens, turkeys, forest birds and thousands of pigeons.

Fr. Cosmas also built a mill to grind wheat and other food for the animals. He made most of the tools in his own workshop, while the rest he was given. They all worked on electricity. He also made another mill to clean corn. Corn can be dropped into a funnel just as it is, straight from the fields, and out of the bottom comes only the kernels. This is a machine of French make. Fr. Cosmas saw it on the farm of some Greeks and, having taken it to pieces, sent them to the G.K.M. Co. to have replicas made. He put the pieces together and the machine was ready. And all this without any money paid to the company, just a few hens, rabbits and eggs.

The cars, tractors and other small machinery of the Mission were maintained and repaired at their own special workshop. They brought in mechanics from outside only for serious damage. They always got a digger from the G.K.M. Co. to widen and level the roads and this was provided free to the Mission. Any pieces of iron, piping, or other odds and ends that were of no use to the company would be taken by Fr. Cosmas and put to good use.

The Facilities and Properties of the Mission

As we mentioned in the chapter on churches, the Mission in Kolwezi now has 15 newly built churches and 3 others, which belong to the Greek communities of Kolwezi, Likashi and Lubumbashi.

The Church of Saint George, Kolwezi, has belonged to the Mission since 1973, and only in the community of Kolwezi is there a Greek priest.

The Facilities and Properties of the Mission

On the tower's 2nd floor is the *kelli* where Father Cosmas lived.

In these three town churches there are cruciform baptisteries. Around them is land, varying in size from 2.5 to 25 acres, which belongs to the Greek community.

The farm and stock-breeding installations of Fr. Cosmas is 1,250 acres in extent, while the facilities belonging to the Mission in Kolwezi are on land of about 25 acres.

At the inner gate of the Mission Headquarters, there are, to the left and right, two towers, about eight meters high, in the form of military fortresses with battlements. Within these are the Missionaries' rooms.

Near the left tower has been built a wing of the mission house, in the shape of an L, the sides of which are 30 × 10 meters. In it is a study room, measuring 3 × 12 meters, for the children, and another eight rooms for dormitories. One room in the middle is the bathroom/toilet and the basins for the washroom are at the end of the building. The kitchens, storage-rooms and children's dining-room are outside the boarding school.

In the autumn of 1988, Fr. Cosmas set about the foundation of the Primary School, the construction of which has now been completed under his successor, Fr. Meletios. Its dimensions are 10 × 72 meters and it consists of seven classrooms, two offices and all the other necessary rooms. It was built in stone, with the arches in brick. All the frames are of iron and are well turned. Before he was killed, Fr. Cosmas had seen to the very last screw.

Apart from this, there are also other places which house an office, the woodwork shop, the icon workshop, as well as two other buildings for the cleaning ladies and the poor and sick.

A little further on is the girls' mission house, where Sister Xeni lives, and the church of Saint Nektarios. Any visitors who come from Greece stay there.

The stockbreeding installations, which are 80 × 150 meters in dimension, have 63 separate areas that are used as hen-runs and to house animals. Outside this large square of stalls and such, three houses have been built, for the stockmen, the overseers and their families to live in.

By 1991, on the vast lands owned by the Mission, about 5,000 coffee trees have been planted, which have begun to yield a crop, as well as thousands of banana trees, and about a thousand other fruit trees, such as mangoes, papayas, avocado, orange, lemon and mandarin trees and others. There are also market gardens, where vegetables are raised for the mission houses and for sale. They also sow corn, beans and wheat for their own needs, for the animals and for sale.

Besides, in the village of Kazambe, there is a building bought by Fr. Amfilohios, where he founded a chapel dedicated to the Holy Trinity. These also belong to the Mission now.

Apart from the above, there are two dump trucks, a Land-Rover, two tractors with all their equipment, milling-machines and other agricultural equipment and many bicycles for the priests to get around their parishes on.

Love of His Fellow Man

Let us now mention some of the works of charity, which we saw and in which we took part. Fr. Cosmas loved the Africans very much and spent himself entirely in their service and for the improvement of their lives. He made no distinction between those who were baptized and those who were not. If anyone asked for help, he made all speed to offer it. Whenever they learned that Fr. Cosmas was around, they ran to meet him and seek a solution to their problems, whether these were of a material or spiritual nature.

He often visited other institutions, found out how they were run and what problems they had to face. First he offered his works of charity to the patients in the State Hospital, who had neither medication nor food from the State. All the poor people went there, because the other clinics were private and they would have had to pay. He therefore gave food and medicines morning and evening to a greater or lesser number of patients, who were not being looked after or supported by relatives. Sometimes the staff of the Mission, with Fr. Cosmas' blessing, cooked for all the patients in the hospital. Any Christians who were ill would first go to Fr. Cosmas, for him to give them a lift to the hospital in Mission transport and also to request that the people in charge would keep them on as in-patients.

Once when they made food for the hospital, I went with them to distribute it. A large number of patients had left, however, and since there was a good deal of food left over, we got into the car to go to the Old People's Home. Away we went over dirt tracks full of potholes, until we arrived at the building, which had neither doors nor windows. There were rats inside as big as cats. We found some old men and women who were in a dreadful state. They made their living by begging. They slept on sacking, without any bed covers. We left them a good many things and Fr. Cosmas told them to go to the headquarters of the Mission now and again to get food to live on.

At the Mission, Fr. Cosmas kept a list of poor people, who once a fortnight or once a month would go there and get a half a sack of flour, sugar, frozen fish and other food. Apart from these, every day there was a stream of poor people, released prisoners, patients from hospitals, people from far-off villages asking for food and money to make a journey, to buy medicines or for other purposes. Whenever Fr. Cosmas left the headquarters of the Mission, he would always fill his pockets with money to hand out to anyone in need.

Apart from the poor and the sick, there were also the prisoners, most of whom had been sentenced for minor offences. If they did not have anyone to bring them food, they would simply die of hunger. Fr. Cosmas went there often and told us their situation was hopeless. For those who had been imprisoned for minor offences, he would pay a sum for their release. The cell blocks were in an appalling state. Very often the prisoners slept in water which came in through the holes in the ceiling. Fr. Cosmas went with workmen and repaired the leaky roofs on the buildings, for which the prisoners were both pleased and grateful.

There were always about 200–250 prisoners in the large prisons. They were always dressed in rags and tatters, and the food that the state provided them with was a plate of boiled greens a week. Many of them fell ill and there was no doctor or medication to relieve their pain or fever. Fr. Cosmas had great compassion for them. He would often take them food with meat in it, while his own doctor would go with him and examine them and give them free medicine besides. He would also give them clothing. To those whose release he secured, he would also give the price of a ticket home, or would take them in Mission transport. He was mainly able to have the poor and sick released.

Another institution to gain Fr. Cosmas' undivided attention was the leper house, which was 60 kilometers outside Kolwezi. He visited them and asked the Roman Catholic priest who looked after them how he could be of assistance. He asked for medicines. He wrote at once to Mr. Papadimitrakopoulos in Thessaloniki, asking him to find drugs for leprosy and to send them. He did, indeed, send a lot of drugs, which were distributed to two leper houses. Today, all those patients have been cured and it is only those who live far out in the jungle who suffer from

Those held in prison showed great love for Father Cosmas, for he did not simply provide them with food. He took an active interest in helping them to solve their problems.

leprosy. He also decided to let them have a pig a month from his farm, as well as other food on occasion.

Wherever he went with the Mission vehicle, he would pick up people on the road who wanted to go somewhere. The truck was often full of people, and he would take them to where they had some job to do. This saved them a lot of trouble, because some of them would have had many kilometers or a whole day's walk ahead of them before they got where they were going.

There were two occasions when I happened to be with Fr. Cosmas. One day we went to the forest near Lake Lualamba, to have a look at the timber and to pay the workers. It was drizzling and two African fishermen, laden with fish, were making their way in a hurry along a path up a slope. Fr. Cosmas told them to wait and that he would pick them up on the way back. And in fact, after we had completed our business, we picked them up and took them into the town. They were afraid to get out of the truck in case the soldiers stole their fish. So Fr. Cosmas took them five miles further out of the town and left them at their huts.

The second occasion was when we were in the town of Lubumbashi. We saw a man curled up at the side of the road. We passed him, since Fr. Cosmas was driving quite fast. Suddenly he stopped and started going back.

"What's up? Why are you going back?" I asked.

He answered:

"That man we saw was starving. Let's give him something to eat so that he can stand on his feet."

We went up to him and lifted him up, though his legs were trembling. Fr. Cosmas gave him quite a lot of money and told him to go to a restaurant to have a meal. Things like that happened every day.

The poor and the hungry who went there always ate in the dining-hall of the Missionary Headquarters. On holidays and feast days of the Church, a table was always spread for everyone. Fr. Cosmas himself would not eat, if all the Africans had not eaten first, because he was so fond of them. He served them with his own hands, and watched to see if they had any other needs when they had finished eating.

On the inside of the front door, there was a special porch with a large cement bench. This was where the sick and poor came to wait for assistance.

Almost every day, this bench was full of our sick and distressed African brothers.

Duties of Judge and Shepherd

The problems of the Africans were many and varied. They were not accustomed to going to court, and the chief of their community or tribe usually resolved their differences.

This was true for the Christians as well. Any problems they had, they took to Fr. Cosmas for him to solve. Very often, a problem was not resolved at once, but some days later, to allow witnesses time to arrive. He always fixed a time and place, and, if for some reason he was delayed, they would wait for him. To get from church to his room after the Liturgy would take more than half an hour. He would speak to one of the congregation, and then another would get hold of him. These were minor instances that could be solved quickly and easily. There were, however, other, more important ones, which he examined through the Mission. His word and his counsels were law for all of them. They would say, "Fr. Cosmas said so" and all hostility and injustice between them would cease.

The most common problems amongst them were disputes, divorces, prostitution, adultery, theft and injustice. He would stop divorces before they happened and would not countenance them. Cases of prostitution and adultery were everyday occurrences. Even after baptism, the Africans had no idea of a moral code and found it very difficult to lead clean, virtuous lives. For this reason, in the catechism lessons he gave the women and the men, Fr. Cosmas stressed this aspect particularly. And in the meetings he held with the younger men and women, he would insist on their preserving the purity of their souls and bodies.

The question of magic was also very serious. Despite having been baptized, the Africans still retained powerful memories of the effects of magic, were afraid that the witch doctor would come in the night and put a spell on them and found it difficult to realize that, after baptism the Devil no longer had any power over their lives through the operations of the witch-doctor. Fr. Cosmas often asked them if they were afraid of the witch-doctor and they replied: "Yes, the witch-doctor is dreadful. He can kill me."

Fr. Cosmas worked very hard to expunge witchcraft from their lives and from their memories. He went round all the towns, the villages, and huts, and into the forest and took away their fetish objects. He collected a great many, and there are still boxes full of them at the Mission. It was his intention to write a book on witchcraft but didn't have enough time. Someone else will perhaps put together a book on the basis of his notes, which would teach many people about the role of witchcraft in those lands and how many lives are lost every day through the activities of witch-doctors.

Samba, the African Doctor

In Africa, sickness and epidemics are rife, so that medical knowledge is of great importance for everyone. Being aware of this, Fr. Cosmas associated with good and helpful doctors, the most important of these being the military doctor, Samba. As far as his profession went, he was the very soul of the Mission. He had some knowledge of almost all specialities. He was a surgeon, general practitioner and paediatrician, and was acquainted with all medical complaints. Together with his wife, who was a paediatrician herself, they were the closest associates of Fr. Cosmas while they lived in Kolwezi, that is, until 1986. He was then posted elsewhere, because, as I said, he was in the Army and held the rank of colonel.

After he had finished his personal duties, he would go and find Fr. Cosmas at the Mission or in one of the surrounding villages, so that he could examine any patients that might be there. They would go together to the houses of the sick, to the prisons, to the workers on the staff of the Mission and to the children in the boarding school, examining them and prescribing the appropriate medication.

Whenever Fr. Cosmas came across someone sick on one of his trips, he would put them into his vehicle, bring them back to Mission headquarters and call the doctor to have a look at them. If they needed surgery, he would take them to the Hospital. Afterwards, he would keep them at the Mission for a few days to recover and then send them home.

Even white people used to go to Samba, because his professional knowledge was greater than that of his white colleagues. And also because he had a noble soul, love and self-sacrifice. A telephone call, night or day, was enough to bring him to wherever Fr. Cosmas happened to want him.

Whenever he heard that a dangerous epidemic threatened, he would take his military team and go to the Mission. He would vaccinate the children, the staff and the workers. His reward was never money. He only got vegetables, eggs and sometimes a rabbit for his family to eat. Naturally, these were provided by the farm.

The Mission Workshops

In Africa in general, and in Zaire in particular, it is not always easy to find what you want. For this reason, Fr. Cosmas set up his own workshops, with his own mechanics, to meet the needs of the Mission.

First of all, he brought in woodworking equipment and set up the woodwork shop. The shop's basic tools were a circular or buzz saw, a plane, a drill and other, smaller items. With these, they were able to make door and window frames, furniture, roofs for buildings and other things the Mission needed to have made out of timber. The workers and mechanics employed there were paid by the Mission itself.

Another workshop was that of the blacksmith. It had three large bottles of oxygen, three electric welders and other auxiliary tools. A trained smith worked there permanently with his assistants and they made anything the Mission needed, such as windows, doors, railings and so on. If they had too much work on and were unable to finish it all, they would give some to Mr. Hambos, a Greek who lived in Likashi, and he would do it for them.

There was also a vehicle repair shop at the Mission. It had all the equipment necessary to repair, clean and change the parts of the Mission's motor vehicles and tractors. Young men trained at the Technical School worked there, but in cases of extreme difficulty, they would call in a specialist from outside.

At the farm there were machines for generating electric light, which worked on petrol, and electric welding machines, which worked on benzene, while all the keys to the machines were kept in the Mission storeroom. There were also spare parts for vehicles and tractors, electrical and plumbing equipment and other things.

There was also an African novice nun at the Mission, Themelina. She knew Greek, as she had been at a convent in Kalymnos, where she had also learned Byzantine iconography and sewing. A few months before he was killed, Fr. Cosmas managed to set up an icon-painting workshop for her, where she worked with her assistants, children from the boarding school.

The Mission also had a pharmacy equipped with nearly all the necessary medicines.

Clothing and shoes were in another storeroom, and were always at the disposal of the poor, the badly-clothed and the ill-shod.

Catechism, Baptism and Marriage

The Mission at Kolwezi had 40 parishes, each of which had one or two catechists whose task it was to teach the true faith to their pagan brothers for one, or sometimes two, years. They taught them the Lord's Prayer, i.e. the "Our Father", the Symbol of Faith (The Creed) and prepared them for Baptism. Some of them excelled the priests in terms of zeal and education, and the fruits of their labours were extremely satisfactory. They kept special lists of candidates for Baptism and gave them to the parish priests. These examined each of the candidates to see if there was a problem with bigamy, if they had handed over their fetish objects and so on. The first question the priest would ask was why the candidate had been attracted to come to Orthodoxy. Then Fr. Cosmas would cast an eye over the lists and only in the cases of outlying districts would he allow the African priests to perform the examination and preparation of the candidates for Baptism.

Baptisms in the villages were appointed to take place in August and September, that is after the seminar which Fr. Cosmas held for the priests all summer long at Mission headquarters. It was very difficult to

Mass Baptism in a river. The simple bridge is made of reeds.

conduct Baptisms in the winter because of the rains, the muddy tracks and the raging torrents.

Baptisms in Kolwezi were fixed for two times a year: Theophany and Pentecost. The number of people at mass Baptisms sometimes amounted to 300 in the towns, while in the villages it was more like 100. It was a principle of Fr. Cosmas' to receive whole families into Orthodoxy, parents and children, to avoid the risk of problems arising later from the fact that some members of the family belonged to a different Christian dogma. After the Baptisms came the marriages of those newly-received, and these were between 10 and 40 couples.

The Order of Service was as follows: On Sunday morning, there was Matins, followed by the Divine Liturgy as usual. The catechumens then donned their baptismal robes and the Baptism Service began, first with the forswearing of Satan and then the espousal of Christ. They themselves

Father Cosmas leads newly-weds in the dance of Isaiah.

responded to the questions of the priest and then said the Symbol of Faith (The Creed) all together in their own language. After catechism, the water was blessed in the cruciform baptistery, the candidates stood around in a circle, the priest poured oil on their heads and they rubbed themselves with it, or were assisted by others. Then came the Baptism in the water. They formed a queue and went down the ladder of the baptistery. They were baptized and then emerged by the ladder on the other side. The priest stood beside them and submerged their heads in the water, while their bodies were already in the water. Once they had all been baptized, they approached the Chalice of Life and partook of the Holy Mysteries, the priest having not consumed all of the Divine Communion after the conclusion of the Divine Liturgy

Thereafter came the sacrament of Marriage for all the newly-illumined couples. The women wore bridal dresses, which they had on loan from

Catechism, Baptism, and Marriage

the Mission, as also the crowns. Because of their poverty it was impossible for them to find such things and keep them for themselves. They kept only their wedding rings for themselves after the wedding. Greek customs intermingled with those of Africa. At the dance of Isaiah, at first they showered the couple with rice, but since this was expensive they afterwards did so with flowers. At the end of the crowning, the others embraced the newly-weds and kissed them on both cheeks. This was entirely new to the Africans, because they had never before embraced, nor was it the custom to kiss even their children.

On the official papers of the State, the old pagan name remained, since it was difficult to change it. Some managed, though, and have their new, Christian name on all their papers.

After the weddings, which finished in the afternoon, a table was laid in the open air, because all of them had fasted since the day before. The Mission provided the food and drink free of charge to everyone.

The newly-illumined were given crosses, usually of wood, as a blessing, as well as anti-heretical pamphlets, while the newly-weds also received a New Testament. All of these were written in their own language.

After the meal, the older Christians would take the new ones and they would start singing. This would last until late into the night and they would also exchange appropriate wishes.

At the Baptism, the Christians were filled with the Grace of the Holy Spirit and really felt the experience of their incorporation into the true Church of Christ. They celebrated this day not simply as if it were an old custom, but as the expression of inner joy and of their redemption from the bonds of Satan. Formerly, when the Mission had given white robes to the newly-illumined, they wore them for a long time to show that they were baptized Christians.

Pascha in Kolwezi.

Liturgical Life and Tours of the Missionaries

Wherever there were permanent priests in parishes, the services were held without interruption, according to the order of our Church. Fr. Cosmas established the practice of celebrating mid-week liturgies, so that those who had no work and were properly prepared could go to church and receive communion. Fr. Cosmas also introduced the service of the blessing of the water, which takes place every month on the Holy Mountain. So outside the sanctuary doors, there would be a font with holy water for the faithful to drink with their antidoron. A good number of Africans attended Matins every day with great compunction, while even more came to Vespers and Compline, because then they were not working. They were very devout during Great Compline and made the familiar prostrations at the prayer of Saint Ephraim the Syrian.

At all the services, but especially on Sundays, order reigned within the church. The men and boys always stood on the right, while the girls and women were on the left, with their babies. They followed the choir in silence and devotion, while the whole congregation sang some troparia together. By the same token, the Lord's Prayer and the Symbol of Faith were recited en masse. The Thrice-Holy Hymn was sung by everyone and at "Thine Own of Thine Own" everyone knelt.

The same wonderful order was observed at the veneration of the Sunday Gospel, at Communion, at the distribution of the antidoron and elsewhere. First the men went up, followed by the boys, then the women and finally the girls. If there were two priests, then one would give communion to the men and the other to the women.

In the villages, where there were no permanent priests and liturgies were celebrated less frequently, the catechist would gather the Christians together in the church on Sunday morning. He would read extracts from the Scriptures to them, they would sing some *troparia* they knew and then disperse to their homes, having reverenced the icons. They were always very anxious for the priest to come and celebrate the Liturgy for them and resolve their various problems.

When Fr. Cosmas went on a tour of the villages, he would celebrate the Liturgy every day, since he had to give communion to some of the Christians and to baptize the infants of others.

He usually sent priests from the staff of the Mission headquarters at Kolwezi to make the tour of the outlying villages. These tours could last up to a month, when there were 5–6 villages some distance apart. Transport was by train, by car if such was to be found, or by bicycle for shorter distances. The priest would send someone to tell the next village that he would be visiting, and almost all the inhabitants would be waiting outside the village to greet him. They carried flowers for him, kissed his hand, spread their garments on the ground for him to pass, greeted him with improvised songs that they had made up for the occasion and thanked him for his love. Then they would all go in procession to the church and the services would begin.

Father Cosmas is met by a village's young welcoming party.

These tours were extremely difficult for white people, because they easily succumbed to various diseases and epidemics. There were lots of bacteria in the water that the organisms of white people were unable to withstand, which is why they boiled water before drinking it. Besides this there were the flies, the mosquitoes, the reptiles and all sorts of insects which were a real nuisance for the more health-sensitive of the whites.

Whenever a member of the staff of the Mission visited villages, they took with them their water, which they had already boiled beforehand, their food, their tents and some medicine. They would pitch their tents near the village and send for the people for catechism, for examination of the sick, and for the distribution of medicines and clothing. It was also a must that they take sweets with them to give to the children.

On the occasions when the Missionaries visited the villages, their hearts were filled with joy and satisfaction. They saw their efforts bearing fruit, they gave and received joy and returned to the Mission Base with many and varied impressions. Occasionally, their trips turned into adventures, in which God had the last word. These visits usually took place before the catechumens were baptized, so that the Missionaries could meet them, get to know them and ask about any problems they might have.

Fr. Cosmas visited villages that were close to the main road from Kolwezi to Likashi himself. Since he often went down to Likashi on a variety of errands, he would fix his itinerary so as to be able to celebrate Liturgies in the surrounding villages. He also served the two Greek churches in Likashi, which did not have permanent priests

He usually travelled at night, so as to gain time. Although the difficulties were considerable, he scorned them all, saying that as a missionary he had to find time for everything. I remember he would often say to Fr. Kyrillos: "Wake up, Kyrillos. Learn all about the Mission, because you'll be left by yourself and you'll be worried that you won't be able to manage." And, indeed, it was not long before Fr. Kyrillos was left alone, without his Elder.

Translations into Swahili

There was no special method for learning Swahili, such as there is for the most important European languages. From the time when he went to Zaire as a layman, Fr. Cosmas started to learn the language, writing words down in a notebook. He would ask the workers in their own language: "What's that?" and they would answer. Then he would write the word down in Swahili and in Greek. In this way, he slowly learned the names of building materials and then liturgical and pastoral terms. This language is spoken in the Samba region of Zaire by more than 10 million Africans.

When Fr. Cosmas went there, of all the Services of the Church he found only the Liturgy of Saint John Chrysostom, translated by Fr. Chrysostomos Papasarandopoulos. All the other services were held in Greek. He tried to find other services which had been translated but without success. Only the Protestants had translated the Holy Scriptures, while on the part of the Orthodox Greeks there was practically nothing. So Fr. Cosmas decided to set about making translations, despite his many other tasks. First he translated the Service of Holy Communion (Preparation and Thanksgiving), both Small and Great Compline and the Presanctified Liturgy. He began a translation of Matins but never finished it. He also translated a variety of anti-heretical tracts and distributed them for free among the Christians of his flock. He was assisted in the translations by the novice Themelina, who knows Greek, and his secretary, who knows French.

It bothered Fr. Cosmas greatly that the people attending services understood almost nothing of what the chanters were singing. For this reason, he would stop 4–5 times during the course of a service and explain what was happening and what he was doing. After the service he would keep them for up to an hour usually, to instruct them properly on matters to do with the life and faith of our Church. He was very meticulous about everything. He took particular trouble to make sure the translations conveyed the exact sense of the original, and would revise his translated texts more than once. It was a great desire and concern of his that the liturgical books of our Church be translated. He would often say to me: "Won't someone be found to translate these books?"

The Recognition of Orthodoxy

The Orthodox Church lagged far behind the other dogmas in terms of foreign missionary work. The Roman Catholics have recently celebrated 100 years of their mission to the natives in Africa. Orthodoxy was first heard officially from the lips of the late Fr. Chrysostomos Papasarandopoulos, after whose death Archimandrite Hariton Pnevmatikakis went from Patras to Kananga in Zaire.

It was in Kolwezi, in 1979, that Orthodoxy became known to the President of the country. The civic authorities had invited Fr. Cosmas to a reception for President Mobutu and his wife. Fr. Cosmas attended,

The Recognition of Orthodoxy

Representing Orthodoxy before the President and the powerful of Zaire.

taking with him a Greek who knew good French. He spoke to the President, who was impressed by his words. Thereafter he was invited to all major events, national celebrations, conferences and so on.

Part of the Kolwezi Mission's good name was due to the construction projects, the building of churches, and, especially, to the farm and stockbreeding facilities. Indeed, when Mrs. Mobutu left, she took with her a few hens and rabbits, as she was fond of them.

The most important thing that the authorities noticed was that the Orthodox Mission did not put out propaganda, but worked guilelessly and charitably for the people's salvation and the improvement of their living conditions. So, all the Africans placed confidence in the Orthodox Church, honoured its work and loved its Missionaries. This can be seen today, after the death of Fr. Cosmas. Every day the Africans go to his grave to pay their respects, place flowers there, weep because they've lost him and remember with gratitude all the good he did them. A military unit headed by officers and accompanied by a band often comes and honours the Greek Missionary who was sacrificed for their country and their people.

There are seven recognized religions altogether in Zaire. The first is Roman Catholicism. Protestantism follows and third place is occupied by Orthodoxy, despite the relatively few years of missionary activity there and the many fewer believers. Then come the other religions, even though they are older.

Bitter Experiences and Trials

We all know from experience that the Devil and slanderers fiercely oppose any spiritual work, since it bears the fruit of salvation. From this rule, Fr. Cosmas was not excepted. As he himself said, he drained not merely cups but "bucketfuls" of poison, without blaming anyone.

The slanderers aimed at destroying his work and turning the priests away from him. They spread the rumour that Fr. Cosmas had embezzled two million drachmas that he had been sent, that he did not concern himself with the material welfare of his priests, that he traded in precious stones, that he sent Sister Themelina to Greece to get married, and that he went to Africa in order to live comfortably on his farm. They even accused him to the then Patriarch of Alexandria, Nikolaos, as being a pig-trader and charlatan.

When the Patriarch came to Greece in 1981, Fr. Cosmas happened to be here, too. They met, and the Patriarch said to Fr. Cosmas: "Is it you who's involved in trading with somebody called Psathas from Kolwezi?" Fr. Cosmas calmly replied: "Come and see for yourself the work I'm doing down there. I work for the Patriarchate of Alexandria and all the property of the Kolwezi Mission officially belongs to your Patriarchate." From then on, the Patriarch highly regarded him and loved him. He even sent him a letter congratulating him on his work.

The devilish purpose of the slanderers was to get rid of Fr. Cosmas. They slandered him to the other priests and forced them to sign a libellous letter against him.

In Lubumbashi they contrived the following way of either getting rid of him or having him locked up for life in prison. Whenever Fr. Cosmas went down to this town, he slept in a room belonging to the Church of the Greek Community. His enemies hung a revolutionary flag above his bed and then went and informed a sergeant to come with a squad of soldiers to arrest him as a revolutionary and enemy of the regime. But God protected Fr Cosmas, and that evening, instead of going to the Church room, he went to the house of a friend, without, of course, knowing anything about what was going on. The next day, one of the church council members went to his room and found the flag under his pillow. He realized what kind of plot had been forged and burned the flag. When he met Fr Cosmas, he told him: "You're fortunate you didn't sleep in the Church house last night. You'd have rotted in the prisons of Zaire otherwise."

Since they failed, they used another weapon: publishing attacks on him. They wrote a lot of things to Greek newspapers against Fr. Cosmas and Metropolitan Timotheos. Fr. Cosmas reacted to all this in the same way: he had been told by his Elder, Fr. George, the Abbot of the Monastery of Gregoriou, not to reply to anyone and that God who watches over us would arrange everything.

A lot of people thought he was making use of the Mission's money and wanted to act as missionaries themselves. So they sent parcels, money and tickets for the Africans to visit Greece. They gave the Africans scholarships, without asking Fr. Cosmas about the suitability of the students or about their background. But they realized by themselves that help such as this would not bring good results, because they were only spending money on isolated cases and not addressing the basic needs of the mission's tasks with responsibility and knowledge of the state of affairs there.

The slanderers realized their mistake and stopped fighting him and calling him names such as "pig-breeder" and "trader." In fact, they asked Fr. Cosmas' mother on the telephone if he would forgive them. In the autumn of 1988, when he was about to leave for Zaire for the last time, I asked him if he had come across anybody he knew and he told me: "I've nothing against anyone and I forgive everybody who did me harm." In the summer of 1988 a missionary conference took place in Athens. They invited Fr. Cosmas, but he chose not to go and told me: "What would I do there? I'll stay in my monastery where I'll have my peace and my prayer."

His Sudden End

In October 1988, he returned to his Base with renewed strength. He pushed ahead with the tasks of founding the school, preparing candidates for Baptism at Epiphany and sending newsletters to friends of the Mission.

At Christmas he was visited by Archimandrite Ignatios Papaioannou, a teacher at the Greek Secondary School at Kinshasa. In the middle of January, he was visited by four people from Greece, Archimandrite Damianos, from the Metropolis of Kassandria, and three of his spiritual children. He took them on a tour of all the sights of the Mission and was very pleased that they had come.

On January 18, 1989, he stood in front of the camera for more than half an hour and spoke to his parents and family about Mission affairs and gave instructions for each one separately. On January 19, he made a video of all the Mission facilities and then left for Lubumbashi with the four Greek visitors. On the way, they visited the churches of Saint Thomas in the village of Karkazembe, of Saint Andrew in Lualamba and of Saint John the Evangelist in Fugurumi. They ate at the house of his closest friend, Mr. Hambos in Likashi and in the morning visited the churches of the town of Lubumbashi: Saint Stephen's, the Nativity, and the Annunciation. He then took his visitors to the airport and returned to

Lubumbashi to do a variety of jobs. He had with him a Greek-speaking African, Moses, who had been four years at the Monastery of Gregoriou, which is where he had learned his Greek, as well as Byzantine music, icon-painting and other things. On Sunday, January 22, Fr. Cosmas celebrated the Liturgy and spoke in church about repentance. On Monday, Tuesday and Wednesday he did all the shopping and ordered the truck to come from Kolwezi to load the things. Sister Xeni came with it. On the way to Likashi, which is about halfway between Kolwezi and Lubumbashi, the vehicle broke down. Sister Xeni got to Likashi by other means and stayed at the house of Mr. Hambos.

Fr. Cosmas telephoned Mr. Hambos, telling him he was ready and was on his way. There was a problem with the gears of his vehicle, however, so he took it to a garage for repair. On those days, Wednesday, Thursday and Friday, he visited the houses of the Greeks, bade them farewell and cried. He advised them on matters of the Christian life and repentance. At the same time, in the three churches in the town he performed services, spoke on matters of the spiritual life and wept. On the afternoon of Friday, he telephoned Mr. Hambos and told him he was coming. He had Moses and the Greek Consul with him.

As the Consul, Mr. Dionysios Kivetos later told me, they left Lubumbashi in rather inclement weather. Fr. Cosmas was playing a cassette of S. Vernados' oratorio "Cosmas Aitolos" and softly singing along with it. They travelled quite a long time. At the fifty-fifth kilometre, where the accident happened, the Consul was listening to the cassette, unconcernedly looking towards the driver (he was not paying attention to the road), while Fr. Cosmas had turned up the volume and was singing louder because the cassette was at the point of the Dismissal Hymn for Saint Cosmas. The time was 8:10 on the evening of January 27, 1989. Coming in the opposite direction was a truck, the trailer of which jutted out some thirty inches on either side of the front cab. Although Fr. Cosmas was a good driver, he didn't take into consideration the trailer's extension. As a result, there was a crash, in which the left side of the Land-Rover, driven by Fr. Cosmas, was literally ripped away. The vehicle turned over twice on the asphalt. Fr. Cosmas was killed instantly. The Consul beside him suffered no injuries whatsoever, while Moses was thrown clear of the vehicle as it overturned, suffered a slight concussion and was taken to hospital in Likashi, from which he was discharged in three days. To this day, the Consul claims that he owes his life to Saint Cosmas Aitolos.

When Mr. George Hambos was informed of the accident two hours later, he set off with his brother-in-law, Ilias, and reached the site. They found Fr. Cosmas lying dead on the earth at the side of the road. The Africans from the nearby village, on hearing the crash, had rushed to help and had taken Fr. Cosmas out of the jeep. Thereafter, Mr. Hambos took him to the Lubumbashi Hospital.

His Grace Metropolitan Timotheos, who was in the capital, Kinshasa, was told immediately of the death of Fr. Cosmas. It was impossible, however, for him to get to Lubumbashi the next day, a Sunday, as there was no flight (and the next one was in two days.) On Monday, January 30th, His Grace Timotheos chanted the Funeral Service in the Cathedral of Lubumbashi, which is dedicated to the Annunciation of the Mother of God. Inside, the church was packed with Greeks and our African Orthodox brethren. The Consul, Mr. Kivetos, was also present. The political and military authorities of Lubumbashi were also present to honour Fr. Cosmas.

Thereafter, his coffin was taken by private aeroplane to Kolwezi for burial in the grounds of the Mission. More than 2,000 Orthodox Africans from Kolwezi and the surrounding countryside were waiting for him. The coffin was placed in the Church of Saint George for public veneration. The Kolwezi authorities honoured him in a most fitting manner: they provided a military guard and the town band. A three-day period of mourning was declared in the town. Representatives of foreign dogmas were also present, as were those of the local religions. All the shops belonging to Greeks in Kolwezi and Lubumbashi closed.

His grave has become a place of pilgrimage for the local people. Every day, dozens of people, Orthodox or not, visit it to lay a few flowers in gratitude to their great father and benefactor. Those who cried most

His Sudden End

The Land Rover in which Father Cosmas departed this life.

were His Grace, his spiritual children, Fr. Kyrillos, Sister Xeni and the African priests.

The sad tidings of his death reached Greece at lightning speed and arrived first at the monastery of his repentance. The holy Abbot of the Monastery, Fr. George, was in Thessaloniki at the time on Monastery business, accompanied by some of his monks. They chanted the Funeral Service for monks at their Metochian of the Dormition of the Mother of God in Stavroupolis, Thessaloniki. There were also two Vigils with Memorial Services for the repose of his soul and special Divine Liturgies for forty days on the Holy Mountain.

The late Fr. Cosmas had many friends and acquaintances all over Greece. When they heard of his death, many bishops and priests cried, prayed and raised their voices in fervent supplication to the Lord Most High for the eternal rest of his soul.

At the monastery of his repentance, as well as at his family home, dozens of telegrams and letters arrived from Greece and all over the

Gathered, celebrating, and chanting in memory of Father Cosmas.

world and continue to do so. Most of them are from people who are unknown to us, who have learned of Fr. Cosmas and his work after his departure from this life.

In a discussion which Fr. Cosmas had with Fr. George and monks of the Monastery of Gregoriou, he told them that: "The Mission isn't only for a few months, and anybody who wants to be a missionary has to leave his bones in the soil of Africa." His words came true three months later.

Fr. Cosmas has left us, but the work of God continues. His venerable Elder, who also wept over him, because he loved him, in obedience to the fervent supplications of the Metropolitan of Central Africa, His Grace Timotheos and after much prayer, sent the Hieromonk and Spiritual Father, Fr. Meletios, as a replacement for Fr. Cosmas.

We hope and pray to the Good Lord that He will enlighten, support, strengthen and sanctify Fr. Meletios and the members of the Mission. The work of Fr. Cosmas and his prayers from heaven will inspire him to

Memorial Service at the tomb of Father Cosmas.

tread the path to Golgotha with self-sacrifice and to bring fruit two-fold for the salvation of our African brothers and sisters.

I hope, from the depths of my heart, that the Lord will grant my son, Fr. Cosmas, rest with the holy Missionaries of our Church and that he will pray for us, that we may find mercy on the day of the Future Judgement. Amen.

Fr. Meletios (right) stands with Fr. Kyrill and another priest at the site where Fr. Cosmas was killed.

Epilogue

THE LAST DAYS
of Blessed Father Cosmas Grigoriatis

By his trusted co-worker, Basil Berberi

Kolwezi: May, 1989

… Father Cosmas has not left us. He is here, among us. He didn't know the meaning of fatigue. When we urged him to rest more, he would answer us: "I will take my rest once and for all, when the Lord calls me near to Him."

It was as if he felt it coming. During his last days he was especially humble, constantly asking forgiveness from everyone—co-workers, priests and the assemblies of the faithful—if, as a man, he had embittered anyone at any time. He spoke continually of death and eternal life, and his homilies at the Divine Liturgy were centered on this theme. He would tease our oldest priest, Father Gerasimos (70 years old), saying: "I will depart this life before you."

Friday, January 20, 1989

One week before the incident Father Cosmas was in Lubumbashi on work for the mission. The day that he was departing the Mission's Base, Theodora, a girl from the boarding-house of the little Monastery of St. Nektarios in Kolwezi, approached him and said: "Father Cosmas, please don't leave, because you'll … you'll die if you go there." Moses, who was present and who would go with him to Lubumbashi, felt his heart constrict at that which he heard and stood looking at Father Cosmas. (Moses is a young native African and spiritual child of Father Cosmas who, upon returning from four years of studies on Mount Athos, always accompanied Father Cosmas on his journeys.) Father Cosmas smiled at that which he heard and, teasing Moses for his anxiety, they set out for Lubumbashi. Three hours outside of Kolwezi they stopped in Likashi to visit a deacon there who was deathly ill. Father Cosmas heard his confession and they immediately continued on toward Lubumbashi. A few days later the deacon surrendered his soul to the Lord.

It was as if Father Cosmas, as I've already said, had a foreboding of his departure. He was continually speaking to us of humility and the love that we should all have for one another. At one point he turned to Moses and said: "If you are left on your own, what will you do?" Moses didn't understand. "What do you mean, "be left on my own," ' he replied, "since we are together here at the Mission?!" "Nothing. Don't worry about it." But later, he said to Moses: "As it regards your Mother's little house, I'll fix it up so that you can also rest easy—so it'll be for you all like a memento from me." Once again, Moses didn't understand what his Elder meant. Today, he knows that his Elder, Father Cosmas, had a premonition of his departure.

Friday, January 27, 1989

It's the day of the accident. That morning, while running the last errands for the Mission, he is informed that one of our two trucks heading toward Lubumbashi, in order to load up whatever he had bought for the needs of the mission, had broken down and was left on the side of the road.

Three times the Greek merchant, Mr. John Hadjilazaros met with Father Cosmas during the course of the day and three times he begged him not to leave that night, since he did not feel good … about him! But, you see, the *ierapostolos* always has work to do and Father Cosmas had become accustomed to travel at night. For, in this way, he avoided the headaches that would come on account of the heat and he saved time, so as to have the day reserved for work and the running about for the needs of the Mission.

So, Father Cosmas, together with the Greek Consul and Moses, set out from Lubumbashi at what was now twilight. It was the will of the Lord to have him close to Him and give him rest, as he himself was saying. And so, as they started out, a certain native trader was traveling with his car toward Lubumbashi. The sun was just setting when he reached the point where Father Cosmas' accident would take place. As he himself related, he suddenly saw a priest ascending before him, from the road into Heaven. He was frightened and stopped his car. Panic-stricken, he called out to the residents of a village that was nearby, that they might also see what he was beholding. No one saw anything except the trader. Finally, full of fear that something bad might happen to him, he decided to spend the night in the village rather than continue on.

Later that night, when the village gathered at the site of the accident, the trader suddenly started yelling, recognizing in the face of the blessed Father Cosmas the priest he had seen, only a few hours earlier, ascending from that very spot into Heaven. Today, all the inhabitants of the village want to be baptized Orthodox Christians. Even after death Father Cosmas saves souls and leads them to our Triune God.

Without us knowing them or they us, that night the villagers watched over Father Cosmas and assisted the other two injured passengers. Furthermore, they didn't tamper with the sacred things that Father Cosmas had brought with him; whereas normally when such incidents occur those passing by usually steal everything. Not only did they not tamper with anything, a few days later they brought us a container of Holy Unction, which Father Cosmas had with him and which was found in the grass after the accident. Here again one sees the hand of divine intervention. In the meantime the news had already spread. Greeks and natives are in turmoil and find consolation in one another.

Everyone, young and old, stayed awake that night. In Greece, everyone was informed, beginning with the monastery of Father Cosmas' repentance, Grigoriou on Mount Athos, and then his parents and others. His Eminence Metropolitan Timothy, Bishop of Central Africa, was informed while in Kinshasa, the capital, and prepares to come to Lubumbashi. The next flight, however, is not until Sunday. So it was decided to place Father Cosmas in one of the refrigerators especially designed for such cases. That night the guardians of the refrigerators see a light around the place where Father Cosmas is being kept and they are seized with fear. In the morning they recount the incident to our priests and everyone together opens the refrigerator. The body of Father Cosmas has not suffered from rigor mortis. They don't understand and confuse things. Some say that the refrigeration wasn't good, others that the refrigerator was probably broken, etc. etc. However, no one stopped to think that a dead body becomes stiff a few hours after the time of death, whether found within or outside of the refrigerator! Thus, what happened is exactly what takes place with the bodies of Athonite Fathers: they don't suffer from rigor mortis and become stiff until after their burial. This, according to our Holy Tradition, is a sign of the love and protection of our Panagia Theotokos for the Athonite monks, for Mount Athos is the garden of the *Panagia*.

Monday, January 30, 1989: Feast of the Three Hierarchs

This morning, in the packed church of the Annunciation of the Theotokos (Lubumbashi) and in the presence of city officials and throngs of people, His Eminence, Metropolitan Timothy of Central Africa, served the Divine Liturgy and burial service. It was midday by the time that the blessed Father Cosmas was taken to the airport. Accompanied by His Eminence and Father Kyrillos, Father Cosmas was taken by plane one hour to Kolwezi where multitudes of people are waiting both within and outside of the mission base and all around the church of St. George. Many of the faithful had spent the previous three nights here awaiting the arrival of Father Cosmas. Such love they had, and they have for him! The people fall in line and one by one, with profound sorrow, approach the coffin of their spiritual father to say their final goodbye. Until we meet again in the eternal life!

Well into the afternoon people continued to arrive from all over, from Kolwezi, from Lubumbashi, both Greeks and other Orthodox Christians, that they might be present at his grave.

When evening arrives, the people accompany Father Cosmas to the place where, as he often said, he would finally find his rest.

Today, our Christians, upon arriving at church, first take a blessing from the grave of Father Cosmas and only then enter into the temple and follow the Divine Services. May God keep the Elder and parents of Father Cosmas, who allowed and blessed him to remain in Africa, together with all those he loved and all those who loved him. We thank them immensely!

Memorial Service led by Father Meletios joined by priests of the Kolwezi Mission, at the grave of Father Cosmas.

Afterword

IN PRAISE AND MEMORY
of Blessed Father Cosmas Grigoriatis

By His Eminence Bishop Avgoustinos, former Metropolitan of Florina, Greece[28]

Some, when they hear they Gospel, say "at that time." "This is written for those of old." Christ, however, is "the same yesterday, today and unto the ages." Our Church doesn't reserve the showing forth of missionaries for the days of old, but continues its mission today, in this harsh, materialistic, new idol-worshipping and Masonic age. In this age of the antichrist we have examples of missionaries both within the borders of our country and abroad.

One such excellent example is Father Cosmas, priest-monk and missionary, for whom we serve the holy memorial today. He lived close to me. He was the child of a poor but honorable family of Thessaloniki. He loved God from his youth. He was a regular at the catechetical schools. He heard the *kerygma* of pre-eminent preachers of the city. He studied much, attending a school for foremen, and could have been an important architect who built houses that would have brought him millions of dollars. Our age is an age of architects, lawyers, and engineers—an age of "how-much-you-mak'n." However, he didn't become such a one as these. Nor did he wish to continue his studies and become a university

---

28 This text was first made public as a homily delivered in the Cathedral of Saint Panteleimon, Florina, Greece, on the occasion of the memorial service for Father Cosmas not many months after his death.

professor, just because he had an extremely clever mind, a mathematical mind. Rather, he preferred the work of the fishermen. He became a "fisherman." He was with us in the early days of great productivity when, together with Father Hierotheos and a few co-workers, we had "hustle it up" as our watchword, and he worked extremely hard.

You see that cross that is at a height of 1020 meters? No engineer would accept the job. Not one. "I'll do it," he said. And with the help of God, he did. Later, when you visit Presva, keep an eye out for another cross that was erected on the blessed little island of Saint Achillius. It was he that labored there as well, transporting the materials by land and sea with much toil and labor.

You see the camps of the diocese? He worked on them. You see the cross in the Sitaria district? He erected it as well, along with the adjacent chapel of St. Cosmas.

He couldn't care less "how much you're mak'n." When he came to Florina and went to the dealers in order to buy supplies, their first question was always: "How much do you make?" They would say: "Being close to the Bishop you probably make a lot. You work on a twenty-four hour basis. You don't have a break, neither on Saturday nor Sunday etc …" He would reply: "I don't make anything, except for room and board." They didn't believe him. They said he was lying. The truth is that the boy abhorred the world of "how much you make," and soon left.

Here let me make a parenthesis. I am thinking of a father who approached a special and holy young man on behalf of his daughter. His first question for the boy was, "How much do you want (as a dowry) in order to take my daughter as a bride?" When he told him that he didn't expect much, the father rejected him as a groom for his daughter. He took another who expected a lot. The boy turned out to be a thief and is now in prison. He doesn't respect the person, but the money. Such is our generation. But the beloved Cosmas didn't belong to this category of men. He was an idealist in the fullest sense of the word. The idea of living in this world of "how-much-you-mak'n" priests and bishops disgusted him, so he sprouted wings, made them grow, gave them power, and flew far away. He made it to Zaire. In those wild places he became an *ierapostolos*. He taught, labored and toiled with all his soul, finding a martyr's death on his way to visit some African Christians, who have greater faith than we do. We are whitened sepulchers. We have Christ on our lips and the devil in our hearts.

The beloved Cosmas was the trailblazer of a beautiful journey for our race. We want to believe that others will follow his example: the feast of a martyr, the imitation of a martyr. Both here in the holy altar and elsewhere there are certain young people who shouldn't become "how-much-you-makers" but idealists. Greece once upon a time had such idealists. Who brought Orthodoxy to Bulgaria, Serbia, Romania and Russia? It was Greek Christians. Nowadays, households don't produce idealists. A child's mother wants him to become a doctor, a lawyer, a teacher, a professor, an engineer, a businessman—anything but a priest. She doesn't even want to hear of it. So it is that today I especially honor the elect disciple, monk and missionary Cosmas. He is a prototype. He is a combination of internal and external mission work.

The servant of God, Cosmas of Gregoriou, *ierapostolos* martyred in Africa to the glory of God and Orthodoxy—may his memory be eternal! And may there be many followers of his heroic example.

Father Cosmas' successors build on the foundation he laid. Far out in the African villages, they teach the Orthodox way of salvation.

Afterword II

IN PRAISE AND MEMORY
of Blessed Father Cosmas Grigoriatis

*By Archimandrite Ioanikios Kotsonis,
St. Gregory Palamas Monastery, Thessaloniki*[29]

Practical and patristic was the ever-memorable Fr. Cosmas Grigoriatis. He was born and raised in Thessaloniki, the mother of holy missions, from where the two Byzantine missionaries Saints Kyrillos and Methodios set out.

He came from a family of fervent Pontians, pious and God-loving, man-befriending, hospitable, and full of the lifeblood and the power of the Orthodox Greek tradition. His father, Demetri, in spite of being blind in one eye, was full of enthusiasm and solidarity for the work of the mission, so much so that he has visited Africa many times. His mother, Despina, heroic and indomitable, who from her bed of illness would not accept sympathy for her missionary son, but prayed rather for a "good resurrection" and sought determined men for the continuation of her martyred son's work.

Father Cosmas was young in age but an old man in missionary experience. He was young in age, but an old man in virtue and *ascesis*.

---

[29] Father Ioanikios is the author of *An Athonite Gerontikon: Sayings of the Holy Fathers of Mount Athos*, published by the Holy Monastery of Saint Gregory Palamas, Kouphalia, Greece. He originally wrote this article in praise of Father Cosmas for *Ecclesiastical Truth* not long after the latter's repose.

He was ardent and pure, vigorous by nature, spontaneous and lively by temperament, full of love, and overflowing with joy, simplicity, humility and meekness.

Representative of things is that which was written by the members of the Mission Corps in Zaire about the creative personality of Father Cosmas:

"He was a priceless treasure. He bore everything with astonishing patience. He was simple, very sensitive, but highly effective. He loved everyone in the same way and sought nothing in return. A radiating spirit, he found practical and accessible solutions for the native Africans. He didn't speak theoretically about diligence and hard work. He disregarded every danger and chose for himself whatever was more burdensome and dangerous. He reckoned not fatigue when faced with bringing relief to his neighbor. Such an ecclesiastical personality, decorated with the gifts of the Holy Spirit—humility, love, strictness, forbearance, diligence—was sure to create a massive work…"

The ever-memorable one was, above all, practical. He exercised the practical virtues in all their spheres. He organized philanthropy. He showed the area of Zaire surrounding Kolwezi to be a model early Christian community where our African brethren were of "one soul and one heart."

Just as the Holy Apostles took care of the sustenance of the first Christians, so did Father Cosmas. Together with his co-workers, by hard and exhausting work he developed a massive tract of African land. A tent-maker, the Apostle of the nations; a farmer, cattle-breeder and builder, the missionary of Zaire. For the first time our black brethren in that area were taught to sow wheat, corn and other useful crops. For the first time they raised flocks of sheep and goats and other animals.

Close to him everyone found nourishment. The all-merciful Lord, "who fills the universe with good will," blesses and multiplies through His servant the "five loaves and two fish." The poor, hungry and tormented people of the black continent—who, for Father Cosmas, are icons of

God—eat and are nourished, first with "daily bread" and then with the Bread of Life "sent down from Heaven."

"Who can relate his countless toils and struggles," writes the Abbot of the ever-memorable's monastery on Mount Athos, Archimandrite George, "for the raising up of the vast apostolic, pastoral and social work?"

For the farming, cattle-breeding and construction work his practical mind had engaged one hundred and thirty native laborers, who were paid from the earnings generated while simultaneously developing love for the practical and spiritual goods of labor. In this way, he managed to create a nearly economically self-powered mission base, something which is not at all insignificant, but rather constitutes the prerequisite of further missionary activity. Within this product-bearing and missionary-apostolic unit he has organized everything: woodworking shop, plumbing shop, blacksmith, storehouses, pharmacy, school, boarding-house, etc.

In his mission group, Father Cosmas had fifteen native priests well trained in their pastoral duties and, most importantly, equipped with piety, dogmatic training and fidelity to Orthodoxy.

The magnificent collaboration with His Eminence Timothy, Bishop of Central Africa, made an impression: the common struggles, the fatherly love of the Bishop and the respect shown him by Fr. Cosmas, who was the Bishop's right hand.

During the last years of his life he conquered the souls of everyone who knew him with his continually sanctified inner world. Father Cosmas was first of all an ascetic and afterwards a missionary. And on this journey he himself was following in the footsteps of the holy Fathers and Teachers of Orthodoxy. He was an Athonite monk and hieromonk who knew what monasticism, ascesis, spiritual combat and the heavenly gifts of fasting, vigil and noetic prayer mean for the Church. He taught the unceasing Jesus prayer as the strongest spiritual weapon against the evil demons and witch doctors who abound there.

An untiring bee—the queen bee in a great hive—the ever-memorable one constantly gave birth to ideas, plans, and a host of children in Christ Jesus, Who "lived in Him." In truth he was both a father and mother to our African brethren, who have by nature a simple, snow-white heart. They loved and adored him, for in his face they saw Christ Himself, as Saint John Klimakos says about the spiritual father and guide. In him they saw the Adorable One of the ages, the Hope of all the nations. For, throughout his life Father Cosmas was able to confess that mystical confession of the Chief Apostle: "I no longer live, but Christ liveth in me."

It wasn't all that important that Father Cosmas had baptized 15,000 African Orthodox. What was most important was that he imparted to them, he united them to, Christ, the Tradition, love, and the liturgical life.

With what longing and eagerness they approached the holy mystery of "regeneration," of Baptism! With what silence and devoutness they partook of the spotless mysteries from his apostolic hands! With what reverential prayer and attention did they enter into and participate in the Mystery of Marriage. This early Christian piety of our native African brethren is a rebuke to us, the supposed civilized Greeks, who clamor and chatter and yet are ignorant of that which is being done and said at the time of the Holy Mysteries.

I have before me issue #108 of the periodical "External Missions" of the brotherhood of the same name from Thessaloniki, which contains the small work entitled "Thoughts on Missionary Work from Experience." This work is a true memorial, an introduction to Orthodox Missions and at the same time a reflection of the great soul of Father Cosmas, who had been baptized into painstaking practice and theory, who had been illumined with the light of Orthodox Tradition and life.

It is a fact that the experiences and thoughts contained within, characterize the ever-memorable patristic and ascetic missionary-apostle. And this is consistent with the fact that he first had the idea to start an Orthodox monastery in Africa. For he knew what an Orthodox monastery means to the missionary efforts. Monasticism played an essential part in the past, from Byzantium until today, in the apostolic beginnings and travels, for monasticism is the ark of the Apostolic Tradition of the Church.

In Praise and Memory: Archimandrite Ioanikios

The apostolic lips of Father Cosmas have ceased to teach and instruct. The apostolic hands of Father Cosmas have ceased to bless. The apostolic feet, which "preached peace," have ceased to plough the African earth. The apostolic heart of Father Cosmas has ceased to beat in the holy altars solidified by his invincible zeal. The sleepless laborer of the divine harvest sleeps in the African earth—in soil that he sowed, loved, toiled over and from which he reaped fruit a hundred-fold.

The tears of our African brethren water that soil endlessly, as if they want new offshoots to burst forth from his grave, runners from a vine stem not dead, which lies in the earth, there awaiting the Resurrection.

The lips of the native Africans, as always when the Son and Word of God is substantiated in the Divine Liturgy, now chant sweetly, with expectation and hope.

In the Mission Center's office, reading a letter. Father Cosmas corresponded often with his colleagues in Greece and elsewhere.

Extracts from

THE LETTERS
of Blessed Father Cosmas Grigoriatis

Sent to His Elder, Father, and Co-workers

Arrival and Beginnings

Kolwezi
January 18, 1979

To His Eminence Metropolitan of Central Africa, Timothy

Your Eminence,

Your Blessing !

" … Briefly, I will try to bring you up to date on the events of the last two months.
    The trip to Africa was good. In Kinshasa, Father Dionysios received me with great love and provided me with assistance so as to be able to depart for Kananga the next day, November 2nd.
    In Kananga, I waited almost an entire month inactive. There, due to the nature of things, it became clear that all that we discussed is inapplicable. Kananga doesn't offer what we need. Thus, I understood from God that I was found in disobedience, for going contrary to the will of the Bishop, who, as the Archpriest, expresses the will of God.

I agreed with the Father Hariton to depart for Shaba, where God was calling me. After a seven day trip I arrived dead tired in Kolwezi. However, the love of the brethren and their desire to continue the efforts of the Kolwezi Mission compelled me to settle in Kolwezi, in spite of the fact that the area is under military rule and lives in expectation of war. The natives received me with great love and they all hope for moral support and solidarity from the Mission…

I have chosen six children (including Andreas) from the nearby villages to live behind the hall where we have rebuilt the old shed with bricks, together with a kitchen.

The program includes theological training, daily services and work for the upbuilding of the Mission. As an experiment we began the cultivation of the building plot of the Mission, transported the appropriate soil and fifteen truck loads of fertilizer (scraps of barley), compliments of **BRASERI**, and we began the planting of the gardens, essential for our subsistence.

In this way the children themselves provide for their own sustenance. In regards to these youth, the Mission is safeguarded by special agreements against any qualms they might have in the future with respect to possible economical demands. Regarding the economical needs of the Mission, let me relate the following.

We've set aside an area of about 200 *stremmata*[30] in Foungouroumi, a continuation of the church's site. All of the necessary papers were filed and it is completely consolidated. In the future I foresee the establishment of the Mission in the midst of a farm…

I am not very enthusiastic about the property in the village of Tsaboula, which is about 120 *stremmata*. Nevertheless, we hauled about 10 truckloads of *toulo*, a special tree for fencing and are continuing with its installation. I chose a large ant colony at the center of the property, the top of which will become a hut for the watchman. When the guard, who will also be the gardener, takes up residence, we will begin to seed various plants.

---

30 One stremma = 1,000 square meters

Dinner with the His Eminence, Metropolitan Timothy.

Without a guard nothing can happen, for the people hunger and, before the vegetables or fruits are able to mature, they will be cut.

The area of the monastery is ideal for large animals, however, I am not sure if we ought to undertake such work today when, with continuous wars, all the animals are devoured.

The brethren began the consolidation of the church properties of the different parishes, and now I am monitoring their processing. It will take some time, for it calls for other, related efforts. With the help of God it will all happen. It's nothing too difficult.

We fixed up a room to the right of the hall, painted it and put all the medicine inside. Please see about getting medicine from the Red Cross, as well as a book describing all the contemporary medicine.

We bought chickens for the poultry farm, as well as goats. I am looking into a property on the other side of Kolwezi for a church and school, in the area of Kasoulou. I think we should buy it and build on it some time later, when the need arises.

Our economic situation you know. Your Eminence, help us to cover expenses for 1979 through *Apostoliki Diakonia* with twenty thousand *drachmas* each month. And this would only cover our food and travel expenses…

Your Eminence, regarding the matter of schools I think that the village of Tsala is suitable, where they have four Orthodox teachers, the village of Foungouroumi with four teachers, and Kamina with seven teachers. After you decide, write me and tell me what you think.

Our parishes are suffering, with our very infrequent Divine Liturgies just barely upholding them. Many are ready to return to their old religions. And this is due only to the absence of priests.

The people are good and warm up when we are present. We have to have ordinations and yet the whole matter is a major problem. The candidates live far away. Write and tell me who you have in mind for ordination so that during the vacation period we can gather them together at the Monastery for the appropriate training, but also to see which 'fish are biting.' From these ordinations I don't think we can expect much, yet nevertheless they are absolutely necessary. Whatever the case, they shouldn't take place short of one year, so as to give them the opportunity to learn the basics.

Yesterday, I invited the three leaders of the heresy of 'the Apostles,' the leader from Kolwezi and two assistants, for a discussion. I presented the theme: 'The Tradition of the Church within the Holy Scriptures.' They originate from the Protestants. They were enthusiastic, saying that until today they had only known of a human tradition, but now see that it is holy, for it comes from Holy Scripture itself. They asked me to speak to them about other subjects. I promised them that I would invite them some other time.

The program of the week includes daily services and Divine Liturgy on Sunday with a homily. After Divine Liturgy there is a catechism class for the younger folks and for the men I give a talk on the temple and Divine Worship. On Wednesday I have a class for a group of young people, fifteen in all, on the New Testament. On Thursday I speak to the men about a series of issues having to do with social injuries (human failings and sins). Sister Anastasia speaks to the women on the same theme on Friday. Each morning we have a study of Holy Scripture and during the week we have two Liturgies, in the church of St. George and in the villages.

All of these efforts help the faithful of Kolwezi and they have begun to follow the various presentations with interest.

I will take care, with the help of God, to maintain this program and, insomuch as we don't have any interventions from tourist missionaries, I hope that things will move forward. I would beg this opportunity to question, even if you happen to find it useful, the arrival at any cost of persons desiring to work in Kolwezi. Your Eminence, we have enough people from different religious convictions experimenting with co-existence. It is better to have one person and a particular task than many with infighting, machinations and calumny, seen and unseen. Mission work is a matter of sacrifice. It demands a total offering, retaining nothing for oneself.

Yesterday, I received a letter from Father Dionysios, who writes me at your command to go, if possible, to Kinshasa in order to replace him. Yes, in ten days or so I will depart for Kinshasa. I hope that I will have your blessing to take Andreas with me in order to assist me with the services, as well as to make possible my communication with the natives there, who speak Lingkala.

I have tired you with my idle talk and I ask your forgiveness.

Your Eminence,
your blessing!
Hieromonk Cosmas Grigoriatis

Like the New Testament

Kolwezi
June 19, 1979

My venerable *Geronda*[31], your blessing!
Beloved brothers, pray for me!

With the return of Fathers A. and Z., I'm taking this opportunity to write you a few lines, for the post is slow, or rather, letters are sometimes lost.

... Again there is talk of war approaching our area. May God protect us. The prayers of the fathers have immediate results for us. I see this every day, not in hallucinations and fantasies, but clearly the hand of God guides us in everything. For example, when thieves will come, what I should do at this moment, what the person I am talking to is thinking. The hand of God encompasses us like an invisible shield, for around us there are not only Christians. There are also wicked, beastly people, witch doctors, and enemies of our Crucified Lord.

Geronda, with regard to the 'spreading out' I agree that it doesn't yet present itself, but the previous situation has left a bad legacy and unfortunately we have to sacrifice a little of our soul's benefit. Whatever the case, I'm following your advice so as to have your blessing and as soon as I feel a little dryness, I abandon everything and, together with the boys, do the prayer rope. It's serious medicine and our only consolation in the monotonous jungle. Every day I remember the answers of Father Auxentius who, to whatever they would ask him, would answer: 'the prayer, say the prayer.' How right he was!

... *Geronda*, when will that blessed hour come when another brother will accompany me toward the realization of the beautiful plans for the founding of a Coenobium? How much a great-schema monk of

---

31 *Geronda* (Γέροντας) means Elder in English.

Mass Baptism in a river. Father Cosmas blesses the holy oil.

our monastery would be able to offer to our little group—even Father Ephraim in his old age! If the council of Elders decided to do this, with his chanting and example he would regenerate souls.

... Father Andreas' desire was fulfilled. I baptized two natives with the name of Andreas. When baptizing I implement the Athonite order of things. We've done 250 baptisms, and, not only with idol worshippers, but also with Catholics who become Orthodox, we baptize them in deep rivers. My actions will have consequences when news reaches the Patriarchate of Alexandria, which holds that the Protestants are only in need of chrism. Until then, however, we will only do Baptisms so as to have St. Nicodemos' blessing.

During the tours we make to the villages I show different slides with a machine I was able to get from Greece. It works using the car battery. It was something amazing to behold in the villages of the jungle. Gathering together people from all the various heresies and dogmas, I would stop at different icons and catechize them on the basis of that which they were viewing. It was amazing.

With our little coenobium we are doing fairly well. The program is difficult, but little by little we are getting accustomed to it.

... I don't remember if I wrote you about your Christmas letter, which arrived about two or three months later. I read it one night to the boys and they really liked it. One of the boys, Andreas, said to me: "Father, that's like the New Testament." He meant its meaning. Yes, I told him, because the same Holy Spirit enlightened then and enlightens now.

I embrace all the fathers and especially those advanced in age. Every time I read their names they pass before me one by one. Then I read more slowly so as to see them better and at the same time I think, will I see them, my older brothers, when I return to our monastery? May God give them a good soul! I beg them to do a knot on the prayer rope for us.

Your blessing.
Your expatriated son,
Hieromonk Cosmas Grigoriatis

The Love and Support of the Monastery

Kolwezi
February 2, 1980

My venerable *Geronda* and beloved brothers and fathers,

Your Blessings!

I am full of joy that our Lord has made me worthy to write you a few lines and come into contact with your love. My letters to the Monastery or the reading of your letters is a great event for me. It is one hour of prayer and spiritual contact with all that Cosmas loves in this vain world. It is true what I write you: I live and breathe within the holy space of the Holy Monastery of Grigoriou. And when I feel exhausted from the weight of my work and the heat of the tropical climate, I take my prayer rope, climb the steps in front of the abbot's quarters, pass through the little door and into the Cemetery chapel or sit outside my beloved walkway gazing at the sea. In this way, at least noetically, I am found near you and under your fatherly care.

When I am found in the church temple for the services and especially for the Divine Liturgy, I join you in prayer and live the unforgettable concelebrating in the *Katholicon*.

All of this compels me to find time and the analogous spiritual state in order to communicate with my Elder and brothers.

On three separate occasions I started to write you and then stopped, because for a long period of time I was exhausted and sick. Things have happened, *Geronda*, which you know about from my correspondence with the Bishop. People deceived by the devil slandered the Mission here in the past. They are doing the same thing now that I am here with your blessings as the head of the Mission, saying all kinds of lies about me. The Bishop wrote me, in accordance with what he had heard, somewhat sternly and I in turn reacted immediately, requesting that the dark methods of the devils be put to an end, if we want to move forward with the work of the Mission.

On this point I ask you to forgive me, for I departed from obedience and placed my ego first, thinking that I would help the work. In the end, with the arrival of the Bishop, all the dark clouds vanished. He recognized that a work of Christ was being carried out and that which he had learned was a lie. At the time, if we hadn't agreed with the Bishop, I was totally ready to return to our Monastery. I was saying in my prayer: perhaps God doesn't want me as a laborer in His vineyard.

During those days I was receiving strength from your prayers, however, and from the letters that arrived one after the other: the periodical *Osios*

Grigorios, the book *Orthodox Tradition and Papism*, the film, my Elder's letter, Gregory's letter, the Christmas package and today, after four months, the letter of Papa Panaretos.

… From time to time, I don't do my prayer rule because I am exhausted. Please write me, and tell me, *Geronda*, if I have a blessing for this or not, so as for Satan not to mock me. Likewise, I fall into the sin of anger with the children of the mission house.

I use the material of your book on Papism often and it helps me tremendously.

I was happy about your trip and the translation of the holy relics of the Builder of our Monastery.

… My thanks to all the fathers and brothers who remember me with their prayer rope, as Father Panaretos wrote to me. Every knot and every prayer brings with it a multitude of blessings for us who live here in the African jungle. Don't forget us. We're asking a knot a day so as to be sustained.

The Bishop is here with us now. He started the ordinations of ten candidates for the priesthood. We've completed about a month of tours and continuous ordinations. Until now there have been seven ordinations… As soon as I have a chance, I will send you the measurements you need in order to sew the 11 cassocks and accompanying scoufia. We thank you!

Your Blessing.
Your spiritual son,
Hieromonk Cosmas Grigoriatis

The Power of the Blessed Baptismal Waters

Kolwezi
February 8, 1981

My venerable *Geronda*, brothers and fathers, your blessings!

I pray that the new year will be blessed and full of spiritual fruits and struggles on behalf of Orthodoxy for our Brotherhood and our Church.

Today we, my father, Mr. Costas Phillipou, some children and myself, visited a village by the name of Kabounzi. The village is found on the border of Zambia (in the area where the rebels operate). We travelled through pools of water and mud on a very bad road. Fortunately, God blessed us and sent us a new car suitable for the forest.

The people rejoiced that we had come to visit them. A priest together with a small choir arrived the day before from another village, so we were able to do Matins inside a thatched hut-church. The Christians, covered with a few shabby pieces of clothing, chanted and sang to the Highest in an Orthodox way. During Divine Liturgy I spoke to them a little about witchcraft, with which they are sorely pressed in this idol-worshipping area, as well as about polygamy, for within the congregation was the ruler of the area with five wives and the leader of the village with two or three wives. Afterwards, the leaders, along with my father and Costas, sat on the stools and began to sing all together, while the women danced modestly in front of them.

I left them some medicine, for different epidemics that plague them, and the native priest remained with them to continue their instruction. We took leave of them and in ninety minutes were back at our Base.

There I found a new, serious problem waiting for me. Exhausted, I had to lie down for a little rest. Yet, the blessing of *Geronda* and the prayers of the fathers always accompany and watch over me. Thus, after a while I awoke relieved and unburdened, having communicated with *Geronda*. I saw him, we spoke a while and it filled me with joy. Unbounded is the

Father Cosmas blesses the water on the Feast of Theophany.

love and providence of God! So many miracles present themselves to us daily, in spite of our sinfulness! May His Name be glorified.

Last month the aggression of Satan toward the work of our Mission Base reached great intensities (testing my endurance). I was obliged to write to different people with a slightly severe tone and, in some way, protested the wrong that was done to me. Of course, some were brought to reason and others answered me with different excuses and justifications. Conclusion: I now understand that it is better to leave aside the mud and the "smears" to my name and to have the reward of one unjustly treated. Forgive me, holy *Geronda*, that the Lord will have mercy on me, so as for me to endure the cross which He granted me for my salvation.

I received great joy from your last letter, which, together with the others, was written from the Vineyard. Your letter written on Papism and ecumenism very much inspired me. It will find a place in history among the texts of our champion fathers who struggled for Orthodoxy.

… With regard to the evil and disorder that Satan directed toward the Monastery, on account of the imminent baptism of the Roman Catholic brother, I have the following to write to you. I have provided a room in the belfry of our church to a demon-possessed woman to stay year-around. She eats, walks, and is generally all right. Occasionally, she starts dancing and singing endlessly, but is otherwise fine. She is advanced in age, unbaptized, of course, and an idol-worshipper. She has nine grown children, but can't live with anyone. With us she calms down. When, however, we have baptisms or *agiasmo* [the blessing of waters], the exact moment that I am blessing the water, even though she is far away, the demon begins to drive her crazy. I have observed this on four different occasions. On two occasions she jumped into the baptismal font. When I asked her why she had done this, she replied that she wants to cast Satan out of her. As this happened right at the time of the sanctification of the waters, both the catechumens and the faithful observed it. So, I preached to them a timely sermon on how the manifest reaction of Satan is proof that the water is sanctified by the Grace of the Holy Spirit. Thus, they are able to use the *agiasmo* with great assurance for the dispelling of the various kinds of witchcraft that are performed against them.

My father and Costas send their regards.
Your blessing,
Hieromonk Cosmas Grigoriatis

Hope Not in Men But in the Lord of the Mission

Kolwezi
January 21, 1983

My dearest and respected Father, greetings in the Lord!

… Father, you shouldn't worry at all about our Mission Center. Satan can war against it with spite or once again take up his offensives, seeing that we are stealing souls from within his kingdom, but our Lord bolsters it unstintingly. I think that during the time that you served this remote outpost of our Orthodoxy, you also gained experience of the everyday offerings of the Holy Spirit.

With regard to your fear that perhaps the various associations will stop supporting us, I answer: when I set out for Zaire I didn't put my hope in the funding of associations, but in the Lord of the Mission. I set out from my monastery with the blessings of my *Geronda* and the other fathers and the explicit command of Father Paisios, who, also, is my spiritual guide, to work together with the heads of the Church for the good of the Mission. The Church exists wherever there is a Bishop and faithful flock. Without the Bishop the faithful do not constitute the Church, but a Protestant heresy. Consequently, the line that I follow, working together with the local Bishop, is the most advisable, and yet even if I wanted to do something different, you know that I wouldn't have a blessing from my monastery, anyway.

You should do whatever you can to spread the idea of Mission and George [his brother according to the flesh] its promotion. Don't, however, do this in order to collect money for us. We work hard with our hands in order to produce whatever we need. If God wants to build a church or school or whatever else, then let Him enlighten the hearts of the people to send it on their own.

I don't want for us to create our own circle of friends of Missions Abroad, as many of our friends would seem to desire. Rather, I prefer for us to support the efforts of *Apostoliki Diakonia*, which is the responsible ecclesiastical vehicle for the work of Missions Abroad.

Father, you shouldn't worry about our work. Everything is moving straight ahead: the catechizing, baptisms, preaching, farming, philanthropy, the enculturation of those at the mission house, the building of churches and schools, the renovation of the new Mission Base, even the clearing of the weeds. Everything is blessed with a surplus.

Pray only that we will have peace in our region, for there are rumors of war for Kolwezi again. It doesn't matter to me if they cut me to pieces or not. That would be an honor and glory for my sinfulness. However, just as every man is joined to the work he offers, so too do I grieve at the thought of the destruction of a work such as this, which has been so blessed by God.

Father, we don't perform miracles, for we are sinners, but at least our work is clean and in accordance with our conscience. I take leave of you, for it is now past midnight.

Blessings to everyone.

Your son,
Archimandrite Cosmas

The Struggle Will Be a Long One

Kinshasa
June 27, 1983

Dear Brother Michael, greetings in the Lord!

You tell me that you are drowning in your work, but come here and you'll see what it means to work.

Of course, the results of our work here will be evident only after quite a few years. For the time being, we can only expend and offer our strength as a sacrifice at the altar of the Mission. In order for a church to be secure it requires many sacrifices from saints, who, with their lives, examples, and even martyric blood, will establish the Church of God in this place, which is now literally ruled by the devil. Until the Lord of the Vineyard sends His worthy laborers, we will stir His forbearance and labor with our weak abilities and passions. Pray only that we not scandalize. We have no talents to offer. The only positive thing is that whatever we do have we give out of love for Christ without holding back anything. Father Paisios tells me: "Continue on, however, the struggle will be a long one, for the people there will be slow in coming to accept Christianity, etc." And his judgments, without him having lived them, I see now, and they are true.

Our efforts our blessed. Catechizing continues in all our parishes. Young native Africans are approaching the Church, but we are a little reserved as to baptizing them. We want them first to be tested well, and this is because we are devoid of staff and good co-workers so as to establish them as baptized Christians in their parishes. With the help of God, in the years to come we hope to be able to take co-workers from among the sixty or so young people we now have in the mission house.

We are battling in Kolwezi to form a small community of faithful Christians with a sacramental life and regular divine services, etc. There are signs of progress. Where we are making no progress is with the parishes at a distance of 300 to 7,000 kilometers.

Our farm provides us with vegetables and other suitable foods (even meat and eggs) for use at the mission house. May God have the glory! It is more than enough for us, so we are able to help out a leper colony, the prisons of the city and quite a few of the poor and sick. The tractor, with which we plough an area of 160 *stremmata* for the cultivation of corn, has helped us in these philanthropic efforts. We are now in the process of making a corn mill to grind the corn, which will take care of a portion of this year's flour.

Over the past few months I have been forced to do all of the confessions on my own. In this I have lived intensely the drama of our fellow men. A large number of the natives here eat but once every two or three days. How they manage to survive is a miracle. They are truly sparrows fed by God.

I am writing you from the capital city of the country. Health-wise I wrestle sometimes with malaria and other times with head pains, on account of sunstroke, etc. "Glory to God for all things!"

Evlogison[32],
Archimandrite Cosmas Grigoriatis

The Problem of Ordinations

Kolwezi
July 5, 1984

My venerable *Geronda*, brothers and fathers, your blessings!

Geronda, I sit down, at this moment exhausted, to write you a few lines and simultaneously to make you a "communicant" in the struggles and the pain for the future of the Church here. His Eminence passed by here recently, full of love and ready to help us in any way he can. He consecrated two churches for us. He appointed a few young women that we have in the mission house (four girls 17–22 years old) to clean their church. He also ordained two sub-deacons, one deacon and one priest.

Here exactly is my problem—the ordinations. I don't see anyone who has some initiative, some pain of heart for the Church. Furthermore, I have to remain continually on alert in order to monitor them. They are always on the verge of falling into laziness or even getting mixed up with witchcraft. If they continue in this way of thinking another ten years, each of them will create their own type of Orthodox worship.

---

32 *Evlogison* in the Greek language is the imperative of the verb "to bless."

I am thinking that, since it is impossible for us to find suitable men from among the adults, we will have to prepare the youth that are growing up under our care. With this in mind, *Geronda*, I thought that you should examine Moses, who you have there with you, if he has the desire to attend the *Athoniada*[33] school and later the Theological School of Thessaloniki, always under the direction and guidance of our monastery.

In October, God willing, I will come to the Monastery for a little replenishment, because I feel awfully tired. We can discuss the matter then, as to how we will staff the Church in this area that is under our care.

If it is blessed, I will bring a young boy who has finished high school to stay in the Monastery for a year in order to learn the Orthodox way; afterwards, a year at *Athoniada* for Greek and then theology in Thessaloniki.

In this way, in a decade there will be, from the ten who will study each year, about fifty who will be able in some way to help the mission. I don't see any other solution.

My father and my co-worker, Captain Basil, send their regards.

Our love to all the brothers, to Apostolos and to Moses as well.

Your Blessing,
Hieromonk Cosmas Grigoriatis

---

33 *Athoniada* is the name of the secondary school located on Mount Athos.

Pentecost Yesterday, Today and Forever

Kolwezi
June 6, 1985

My dear Father,
Rejoice in the Lord always!

Chronicle for the Feast of Pentecost 1985

Saturday June 1, 1985

… On this day, from daybreak until midnight we performed the baptisms of one hundred catechumens and the weddings of ten Christian couples… In the evening, the women kept "vigil" in order to prepare tomorrow's table with food and a pig that we brought them. There in the courtyard of the church six Christians from the village of Bade also spent the night. These are the first leaven of Christians from their village. Along with them there are also twenty-five others from the town of Kampoube, also the foundation of a new parish.

Sunday of Pentecost, June 2, 1985

The first spots in Likasi's Church of the Three Hierarchs were filled from beforehand by the newly wedded and further back the newly illumined. They followed the Divine Service with great devotion and partook of the Body and Blood of our Lord for the first time. The "brightness in their faces" at such moments is beyond description, but is a reality which we live and from which we receive strength in order to surmount the array of daily difficulties.

At midday old and new Christians ate together sitting on the ground. They ate with their hands, without settings, but with simplicity of heart, much joy and the Grace of the Holy Spirit. The Pentecost in the Upper Room of the Disciples of our Lord, for the one hundred newly illumined and for us who took part in this celebration, continues today just as it did then. In the afternoon, Vespers with the Kneeling Prayers took place, with the van taking the twenty-five newly illumined to their village a little later on.

Monday of the Holy Spirit

At 6 am, Matins, followed by the Divine Liturgy. We have a gift of God in our co-worker and friend of the Mission, Mr. Hampo from Cyprus, who sacrifices himself in order to serve us whenever I go to Likashi. On our return we drop off the family of a catechumen at the village of Bade and by mid-afternoon we arrive in Fugurumi. We leave Father Romanos there and load 5 tonnes of corn for the feeding of our mission boarding house.

Late in the evening we arrive in Kolwezi. Here I found Christopher, one poor Christian, carrying his dead five-year-old son on his back in order to go to his village, which lies ten kilometers outside of Kolwezi. In the span of two weeks this man lost five children from an epidemic. I took him, his son and his wife in the car to the Mission Base. We put the poor little child in a coffin, covered him with a white sheet and, together with Father Gerasimos, took them to their village in order to bury him. Outside of their hut both Christians and idol-worshippers were waiting for them. The later group started to mourn in their usual way, bent over and rolling on the ground, belting out inarticulate cries. We calmed them down and read the Service and spoke to them about death and the Resurrection. Father Gerasimos remained with many of the Christians in order to pass the night with chanting and prayer.

A little tired, I returned in the middle of the night to my cell, where my assistant, Father Kyrillos, awaited me in order to inform me of the problems that arose during my absence.

Our lives down here in the heart of the Black Continent follow this pattern of things. We work night and day, contending for the glory of our Lord and for our dearest Orthodoxy.

With the love of Christ,
Archimandrite Cosmas Grigoriatis

Pastoral Discernment

Kolwezi
October 20, 1986

My venerable *Geronda*, brothers and fathers, your blessings!

These days I see that the evil one is trying hard to destroy us: serious damage to the automobiles, friends suddenly become the worst enemies, worries and anxiety from our co-workers, many times without justifications, etc.

So it is that I withdrew to my hermitage and placed myself on a strict fast, as many days as I can withstand, purification of heart with continuous study of the appropriate books of the *neptic* fathers.

... Beloved *Geronda*, I am sending you my program and awaiting your blessing or modifications to the program. In any case, one thought that I have is that, if I don't have internal indication of illumination and the prayer in my heart, I shouldn't go ahead with the evangelization of the people. Even though the place is ideal and there is grace, I am not managing it in the prayer. Please pray concerning it and write me.

I have the wireless with me and even though I am far from the Base I am able to stay on top of the work and give the necessary directions, for the mission has grown tremendously and requires close guidance.

... If God desires it and you bless it, around Christmas, along with Father Kyrillos, I am thinking about sending you Father Iakovos, a native priest who oversees the parish in Kolwezi, so as to partake a little of the nectar of our Divine Services, which he loves so much... He is different from those I have sent you so far and I believe that you will be encouraged by him to send us two or three fathers toward the building-up of the Mission and for the sake of souls. It should be noted that, before he was regenerated in the waters of Baptism, he was a wild beast that no one dared stand up to. Such are the miracles of God.

With regard to certain pastoral matters I would ask you to write me your opinion, not so much as it pertains to the canonicity of things, for the position of the Church is most likely known to me from the *Pedalion* (Book of Canons). I am asking mainly in order to learn, from the perspective of *oikonomia*[34], to what degree we can acquiesce.

There are a large number of women, who live with men or have gone through ecclesiastical marriages, who nonetheless have husbands that have another woman or many women in the same or another house (polygamy). The questions are 1) Will these women remain catechumens for life? 2) If they are Christians, will they remain non-communicants? 3) Our counsel to dissolve the marriage has a consequence: abandoned children in the street and new illegitimate relationships. 4) In the case where they both do obedience, a solution is reached. Otherwise, there exists a major problem surrounding the issue of polygamy.

Perhaps, in the circumstances above, 1 Cor. 7:13 might not be applicable.

Circumcision is practiced here, being handed down by their ancestors. That is, it is a part of their customs and creates problems with their grandfathers when Orthodox parents refuse to circumcise their children. Is it

---

34 *Oikonomia*: the pastoral application of the canons by the priest.

good for us to insist that they stop circumcising or is it inconsequential and should we leave them to do as they wish?

Concerning the eating of rats, snakes, apes, grasshoppers, worms, etc., besides questions of health (since it doesn't matter much to them), should the practice continue as it has?

Regarding the matter of theft, which a man does here in order for him and his children to survive, what position should we take? (I read recently that a major synod of Roman Catholic Bishops in Latin America judged it not to be a sin and sent their conclusions to the Pope.)

Geronda, if someone asked me the above questions ten years ago, while I was still living in Greece, I would have been uncertain as to whom to direct the questions. Today, however, living the problems of the Africans here where they happen, I consider it very natural to direct the problems that I confront on a daily basis to you. Please transport yourself here noetically and whatever God enlightens you, write me and we will put it into practice.

Father Kyrillos and Sister Paraskevi ask your blessings and send their regards.

Your Blessing,
Hieromonk Cosmas Grigoriatis

"Go ye therefore, and teach all nations, baptizing them in the name of the Father, and of the Son, and of the Holy Spirit; teaching them to observe all things whatsoever I have commanded you; and lo, I am with you always, even to the end of the age."

Matthew 28:19-20

Extracts from

THE BOOK
of Blessed Father Cosmas Grigoriatis

Thoughts About Missionary Work from Experience

The Place of Action

Before we arrive at the place of action, the missionary, or a co-worker on the front with him, would do well to study and learn elements of the place of work. These are summarized as follows:

a. Official, and local, language.
b. Environment, climate, elevation, high and low temperature.
c. History of the country ethnic groups in general.
d. Ancient religion, contemporary creeds.
e. Ethos, customs and traditions. The good elements should remain, the pagan elements should be christianized, and the bad should be removed.
f. Characteristics of the ethnic groups, as well as the differences, oppositions, and contentions between them.
g. The existing missionaries of other dogmas who are at work, their extent and numbers of faithful, years at work and relations with the Orthodox mission.
h. Sicknesses, epidemics, and their confrontation.
i. Place of residence, grounds and quarters.
j. Political succession and contemporary regime.
k. Sympathy or bad disposition of governing party toward Christianity.

1. Existence of fellow countrymen, distance from the mission base and total number. This factor is primary, especially at the outset of the mission. Saint Paul, at each new city that he came to, met and associated first with his fellow countrymen. Likewise, blessed Father Chrysostom Papasarantopoulos employed, at his outset, the fellow countrymen of Kolowezi. He had as a base the house of the most pious Christian, Mastoridi, for the first contacts with the native populace the shop of M. Psatha, and for transportation the family of Hatzilazarou, etc.

Another basic element that the missionary must be conscious of is the abstention from all political propaganda and intentions. Keeping his political beliefs strictly to himself, let him help the African become a good Christian, and he himself, on his own, with the passing of time and divine enlightenment, will choose and pursue that which is in his best interests in the political arena.

The Human Dynamic

From the outset, the missionary must know well the human dynamic with which he will work. It is not sufficient that he merely have a good disposition, without knowledge of the people, for otherwise the multitude of his daily blunders will gravely disappoint him. More to the point, he must examine just who the natives are: whether they are malevolent or benevolent; what conflicts exist between the different tribes; their little wars, vendettas or rebel groups; the degree of their attachment to the witch doctors; their tenacious or weak belief in the idols and ancestral spirits; the level of their culture, conditions of life, loose or strong family ties; the percentages of alcohol and drug consumption; their submissiveness or rebelliousness, the degree of sincerity or deceit, etc. Based on these elements the missionary orders the appropriate plan of action and his general demeanor.

The new missionary must know to commit himself only to that which he is able to reciprocate straightway or in the short-term. Long-range or unfulfilled commitments create great problems. Likewise, he must preserve tempered trust in his native co-workers, for their inconstancy and capriciousness is a given. And something important: if the missionary loves and truly wants to help the native believer, let him not show his love through familiarity or closeness, but let him keep a distance, something that substantially helps him.

The Means and Manner of Conducting Evangelism

A good and studied beginning ensures more success. It demands a program and preparation made with care, orderliness, and peace, according to the words of the Apostle: "Let all things be done decently and in order" (1 Cor. 14:40). This protects the missionary from future pitfalls and pointless labor.

In every missionary endeavor the laborer of the Gospel is obliged to know "from the outset" the aforementioned in the "Place of Activity" and "The Human Dynamic" chapters, simultaneously examining the method and means by which they are suited to his character and circumstances. Four approaches come under consideration:

a. Beginning catechism and baptisms in the countryside and working toward the centers.
b. Beginning catechism and baptisms in the centers and working toward the countryside.
c. Use of philanthropy as a means of conversion.
d. Beginning with the liturgical, life of worship, for the manifestation of Orthodoxy to the pagan world.

Each missionary, in consultation with his local bishop, regulates his mission group based on the above methods or a combination thereof, giving to the work its own style and color. This, of course, happens over time. With the passing of time, the work takes on the complexion of all those who labor therein. In this respect, the work is a linkage of one's own temperament, knowledge, possibilities and local conditions. It is not necessary to follow certain molds, nor for someone coming from such a mind-set to be considered unorthodox. The missionary is free and when he is open to the grace of God, the Holy Spirit will speak riches in his heart and indicate to him what to do, gradually and in correspondence to the development of the work. Let us leave room for prayer to act, without rushing the situation with narrow logic, absolute measures or the assessments of critics at each stage. Such grievous criticism wore down and extinguished the persecuted, blessed Father Chrysostom.

From the Countryside to the Center

For many different reasons, the commencement of evangelization might begin from the countryside, from the rain forests, when, for example, the centers are held by other dogmas or the official state doesn't allow entrance into the large cities, or even when the outlying areas offer more access, due to the existence of fellow countrymen who are businessmen or old groups of Orthodox… To the degree that the work is known to be and presents itself as upright and pure in the eyes of the natives, the missionary endeavor is propelled toward the center.

From this point, however, until its implementation in our own days, "a great chasm exists." To give a specific example: A small missionary group travels by car through the tropical areas and stops somewhere to eat. They see five huts in that place, give a few gifts to the natives, baptize them and then leave them to the mercy of God, without instruction and without a priest. The next day, again at a distance of a few hundred kilometers, they baptize another fifty people. Over time we see around us, in an area the size of Greece, the existence of ten or so parishes, without

Divine Services or a priest, with neophytes fit to fall, and all the while we talk of making all the Africans into Orthodox Christians.

This example should not be held up as a standard, nor is it worthy of imitation. I live the reality and I urge the neophyte missionary efforts not repeat the same mistakes and disorders, which, as the Scriptures say, are not pleasing to God: "For God is not the author of confusion but of peace" (1 Cor. 14:33).

With sadness, however, I observe that the very same method is being practiced in other Dioceses. Therefore, if in the near future a missionary with zeal assumes the work, and not just as a tourist, he will find himself surrounded by a thousand and one problems, with no way out, not knowing where to start and where to end. I would strongly urge any future missionary, bishop or priest, who may have to take over such a diocese, to begin his own well thought-out endeavor, without many distractions, assigning the old work to his assistants, monitoring it to the extent that time is made available from his own work. He will take up the old work after a decade or so, when it has acquired its own staff that will assume the vast and unsystematic work. Otherwise, speaking from personal experience, the missionary will run from village to village, struggling greatly without fruit and the native will remain without a shepherd.

From the Center to the Countryside

It is clear that, if someone is supported by major economic support, he is able to fearlessly employ the method of going from the center out toward the countryside. This is preferable to the first method, for in the first method one sets off with the Gospel alone.

The first concern is the finding of an appropriate, centrally located, if possible, site, where a spacious church and living quarters for the missionaries can be built. (If there are also female missionaries, a second building for living quarters can be built at a short distance from the first.) Likewise, a rudimentary medical clinic, working space and meeting hall are all necessary. Catechism then comes next. From the neophyte believers are chosen the first co-workers. According to time constraints and the development of the work, catechists and priests are prepared and trained. When all is ready, the radial decentralization of the staff begins, orderly and according to a plan.

This method was put into practice with good results by Father Chariton Pnevmatikakis at the missionary center in Kananga.

Philanthropy

Methods of philanthropy (hospitals, first aid stations, educational centers) have been implemented to the point of saturation by other dogmas. The results, however, show that the method does not yield as much as the work offers. I have met hundreds of natives who were forced to approach baptism in order to be educated and accepted at one or another heterodox school. They remained Christians as long as they were being educated. Later, they became indifferent, returned to their old religion or joined another heresy, in so much as every ten natives means a new heresy. Over three hundred heresies exist in Zaire. In my opinion, therefore, the method of philanthropy [for conversion] is not advisable, at least in the beginning. Over time it may be possible to use it as a secondary method, like a capping stone.

The Life of Worship

The best method and means, in my opinion, for a sure and tested beginning is that which the missionaries of Russia have implemented: the building of churches, the settlement of missionaries and, most preferable, the installation from the outset of a monastery with coenobitic life.

In this approach, the native draws near and observes, at first out of curiosity, and over time becomes a believer and is educated, workers are prepared and trained, and the Monastery is filled with native novices, and the work gradually flourishes… A basic presupposition, however, is that the first monks or nuns of the Monastery have monastic experience, holy life and divine *charismata* (gifts from God), like those of the Russian Church, otherwise it is in danger of failing.

Challenges to Evangelism

Living among the simple and humble Africans, I observe that Orthodoxy, with its living Mysteries and liturgical brilliance and spirituality, fits better than the other dogmas into the spiritual world of our African brothers. The Africans, with their mysticism, their introvertedness, their ancestral worship and their godly piety, constitute fertile spiritual ground for the Orthodox teaching. In our effort, however, to place different inventions of the heterodox upon the simple face of Orthodoxy, we labor at the width and not the depth…

Syncretism

Recently, in one of our magazines I saw that in one diocese there are groups of natives approaching Orthodoxy in places where an Orthodox missionary has never set step. These groups comprise organized heresies of religions with leaders, etc.

Having personal experience of the phenomenon, I know that the entrance of these groups into the bosom of the Church enthuses us due to their numbers. In reality, however, these groups turn out to be very problematic and never become truly Orthodox. They are possessed of a spirit of syncretism, and that is why they do little of what we propose to them, and all the rest, from their old religion, basically, is satanic worship. Thus, Orthodoxy for them is a legal umbrella, cover and showcase, and not something essential. In this regard, I remember the words of Father Paisios, who told me that, most of the time the baptism that the heretics perform only passes over their skin. I think some similar syncretistic phenomenon happened during the evangelization of the Far East (India, China, etc.) in the first Christian centuries. That is why today, in the depth of certain eastern religions, one can see the glimmer of certain Orthodox elements…

… Obvious proof that one such group was not interested in our Faith, is the following event: when, on account of [canonical] impediments, we refused to ordain their old leader, they all left en masse.

We received new proposals for them to return, once again in mass… We answered them that we accept them under the following terms: that they enter the catechetical program one by one, and not as a group, with leaders. The few, who are free, entered unconstrained. Most went back, returning to their old habits.

These contemporary syncretistic groups, with their Orthodox baptisms, will be only a good memory for the future. The guise that they will take later on will be anything but Orthodox, if they remain without a non-African missionary to shepherd them.

As regards their present spiritual father, he cannot be excused on the pretext that he did all that he could, shifting the responsibility to those who could have but did not come to help. The Apostle Paul, if he did not have co-workers to leave as bishops in new areas or if others were journeying, did not continue on, but remained quite a while in such cities to oversee the implanting of the new faith.

We must not advance without co-workers. We must not believe that, with our example and sacrifice, probably admirable, we will move others to join us. These are realities of other ages and other peoples; today, among our people, almost all of us are prisoners of comfort and individualism.

Nevertheless, there is a light, a hope that shines on the new monastic brotherhoods, but it will be slow in coming, for the fathers, still young, must first be strengthened and tested, as gold in the furnace, in the coenobium. There will be those who will receive the gift of grace and information, such as St. Cosmas Aitolos and Saint Maximos the Greek, to come out of the Monastery with humility and obedience for evangelism, planting and watering patiently in the pasture of the Lord.

Today's Colonialism

The effects of today's colonial spirit are even more damaging than previous ones. The African believes that he has gained freedom, but in reality he has sunk to a lower level than before. Seeing that things have gone wrong, the nations' businessmen, while apparently not interfering in matters, have introduced another, third form of colonialism: the computer.

Under such oppressive treatment, the simple African is disfigured, he is changed into a weaponless revolutionary with no conscience, who hates everyone and everything, not knowing whom or what to strike, receiving blows and injuries from all, until, having lost his orientation, he finally loses his identity.

In this psychological dead-end in which the African finds himself, he wants and needs to be helped to find his divine roots, to find peace for his soul, to be united with God, to love his fellow man, and then, in peace and quiet, to make his own decisions about his future.

The Role of Orthodoxy

All that I have mentioned above, about the spiritual equilibrium of the African, will be given him by Christ through Orthodoxy, which dispenses the spiritual pledges and is uncolored by politics. Today, the African looks with suspicion on the religion which has been associated, well or badly, with the conqueror, and therefore he is more open to Orthodoxy. This will lead him in the end to the true path of salvation.

Let me repeat something which I mentioned before. It is wrong to have recourse to the means and methods of the heterodox. Let us leave to Orthodoxy her own color, in faith, in teaching, and in Her art. Let it not

Victory in the Death and Resurrection of Christ Jesus.

fade in the mission field. In an Orthodox manner, humbly, coenobitically if you will, without displays or cosmetics, let us not uproot the African from his place. It is preferable for us to enter his world, and there to find ways and means to adapt Orthodoxy, not in doctrine, but in mode, so that the newly-enlightened will feel at ease, acclimated to his own land, and furthermore, overshadowed by the grace of God.

It is not necessary to inoculate the African's body with our own civilization, with all its attendant cancers. The African has his own, very noteworthy civilization, his own social structure. The missionary must labor greatly to discover it and Christianize it.

Interview

ORTHODOXY AND MAGIC ON THE BLACK CONTINENT
with Blessed Father Cosmas Grigoriatis

Conducted in Cyprus months before his repose

Interviewer: Father Cosmas, you are a part of the Foreign Orthodox Mission in Africa of the Holy Monastery of Grigoriou on Mount Athos. In Zaire, where you are, there is widespread practice of witchcraft. How do you understand this phenomenon? How does it work? You must have quite a few experiences to relate for us?

Father Cosmas: Witchcraft is one the very basic problems that the missionary confronts. Afterwards, there comes polygamy, drunkenness and the other passions. I have many personal experiences of these from my life down there, from confession, exorcisms, and everyday life.

There are two forms of magic or witchcraft—black and white. When we speak of black magic, we mean blood and death is involved. White magic is performed by him who seeks to expose the evil magicians. The black magician is called "Moulozi," whereas he who performs so-called white magic is called "Moufoumou." The Africans consider the white magician to be good, for he helps, he gives the medicine and exposes the evil sorcerer. Both of them, however, work with the same means, the same powers—demonic powers. They simply toy with the people, playing one off against the other and vice versa. And in this way, practically the whole of the African world is clutched in the hands of Satan, the hands of the magician and his witchcraft. To put it simply: I would say that the magician or sorcerer is he who runs the African world.

Magic, of course, doesn't exist only in Africa. Recently, when I was on Mount Athos, quite a few priests came to discuss different problems they face in their parishes. White magic, that which basically exists in Greece, can start from a simple coffee cup, in which they will see people's fate, and advance to more serious forms of magic, such as cups which float, tables that move and spiritualistic mediums.

Black magic is not fancifulness or extravagant notions. It is something that the native lives and is literally governed by. In the village, for example, no one dares speak about the magician, for he fears that something bad will happen, either to him or to the village in general. I have seen first hand what they mean…

Interviewer: In other words, there are clear cases of Satan-possessed people?

Father Cosmas: Unmitigated. They have many and diverse powers, such as murdering a child in the womb of his mother, redirecting lightening, making you see fire in front of you, etc.

Interviewer: You're saying that they have certain powers, these people?

Father Cosmas: Very great ones. I am making a study now of witchcraft. At some point I want to write something, after having collected enough material. In this process I have met many people.

Interviewer: Do they call upon the powers of evil? Who helps them? The evil spirits?

Father Cosmas: They call upon Satan, of course. The sorcerers do unbelievable things, up to and including murder. Satan helps them. However, after they have been around for a while Satan himself comes and extinguishes them. In other words, these people self-destruct. At the end they are found in a very difficult position.

I have cases of major magicians who have come and sought refuge in Orthodoxy. First of all, they hand over their satanic tools—I have sent some of these to a museum of mission work in Thessaloniki—and little baskets, which are filled with different items, pieces of human bodies, effigies of animals and other different items. They follow a certain process and are finally able to attend catechism class. When they are baptized they are completely delivered from the nightmare, which day and night prevents them from finding peace. All of this, of course, is with the presupposition that it will be preceded by purification and confession.

Interviewer: In other words, repentance. Father Cosmas, there must exist special prayers for such cases as these. What prayers are these and how are the possessed dealt with?

Father Cosmas: The prayers of those written by Saints John Chrysostom and Basil the Great, as well as several very good prayers by Saint Cyprian, who was himself a magician and knew many of the magicians' secrets. I saw for myself, down there in Africa, with the many incidents I have seen, that each word that is said in the exorcism of St. Cyprian constitutes a separate type of witchcraft.

Interviewer: Are there books on magic and witchcraft?

Father Cosmas: They don't have books. They are all initiated orally amongst themselves. A young man who had killed his sister's children and, finally, wanted to become Orthodox, told me that his grandfather had initiated him when he was a little boy. He took him to some river, they sat on his left and his right, lit fires and performed their religious ceremonies. Generally, sorcery happens at night, sometime after midnight. The missionaries celebrate a nighttime Liturgy, after midnight, especially for the magicians, in order to immobilize them.

Interviewer: And Christ cast out demons from the possessed.

Father Cosmas: Certainly. God, of course, is all-powerful and through the Mysteries of the Church the magicians are totally brought to no effect. We often go to the villages and celebrate the Liturgy and afterwards the Blessing of the Waters (*Agiasmo*), which drives out the witchcraft. They have their own "*agiasmo*" and their own instruments. But the Church is very strong, which even the magicians themselves admit.[35]

Interviewer: Are you afraid of them at all?

Father Cosmas: Certainly not. That's not even an issue. The natives, however, have yet to develop the faith that will enable them to not to be riddled with fear.

Perhaps at one time they themselves have served magicians before being baptized. They are members of these communities, grew up surrounded by magic, believing in it at one point themselves. Many generations will have to pass before they will be able to forget such things and be able to confront them, as we are able to confront them.

Interviewer: Father Cosmas, you said that magic and witchcraft happens in Greece and elsewhere. How does our Church deal with such cases?

Father Cosmas: There is certain magic by which families are broken up, people become anemic or even die. It is necessary, if the problem exists between a husband and wife, for both of them to hand over their objects (for there are certain powders, bottles, bones, hairs, soaps, etc. which are used). Afterwards, they must both accept in confession that they sinned, repent and seek the help of God. And then the exorcisms are read. Usually, as it happens here in Greece, only one of the two approaches the Church, while the other remains in their sin, and thus the problem remains unsettled.

---

35 See story "He is Greater than Me" on pg. 169.

Orthodoxy and Magic on the Black Continent

Interviewer: How is the person helped who suffers from an attack and may be innocent?

Father Cosmas: Innocent people and good Christians are not affected by the magicians. I have in mind particular cases of newly-illumined Orthodox who I baptized and who became objects of the magicians' attacks, but they couldn't do anything to them.

It's a given, for me anyway, 100% of the time. No magic of any sorcerer can touch the conscious Christian, who makes a clean confession and receives Holy Communion, and who follows what the Church tells him. A humble mindset, of course, is also necessary. At a lecture I gave in Athens one woman rose up and said: "I dare the magicians of Athens to do their magic on me!" I explained to her that it was not right to say such things. "But, since I confess and commune what do I have to fear," she answered me. The egotism that someone who says "I dare," has, is sufficient to provoke the demons and she could be found in serious trouble.

The conscious Christian, however, with a humble mindset, is armor-clad by the grace of God and no witch doctor or magician can do anything whatsoever to him.

An African symbol meaning: the present generation ought to respect the wisdom of the past.

Father Cosmas' successor, Father Meletios, joined by the priests of the Kowlezi Mission, during the month-long seminar held every summer at the Mission Center.

THE LEGACY
of Blessed Father Cosmas Grigoriatis

By Monk Damascene Grigoriatis

In the pages that follow, I will endeavor to set before the friends of Orthodox Mission the miraculous signs attending the history of the mission during the times of Father Cosmas and his current successor. I thought it necessary to put into writing and so rescue from oblivion the various facts and episodes which constitute the recent history of our mission, to the glory of God and the spiritual profit of those who read it and those who may support our work.

Reflections on, and Incidents from, the Life of Blessed Father Cosmas

Help Provided to Travelers

Father Cosmas was of the firm conviction that God had sent him to Africa not simply as one sent by the Orthodox Church but as a man of love who would sacrifice himself for each man regardless of race, nationality, skin color or religion. Thus, wherever he happened to be, if he saw that people needed his help he didn't ask whether they were Orthodox or what religion they practiced. Rather, he helped each according to his need.

From the "Chronicle" that he kept I was able to glean some snapshots of his humanitarian work and sacrifice. Father Cosmas would often stop his car and use his cable to tow the poor African villagers' pushcarts, particularly if it was a steep incline. If he saw that a car was stopped

His love for God and man extended to include all creation.

on the side of the road, he would ask what the problem was, put on his work clothes and slide underneath it in order to repair it. If the car had run out of gas, he would personally return to the Mission center, fill a container and return in order to help his fellow man.

One time, one rainy day when Fr. Cosmas had gone with his father to the forest which borders on Lake Lualaba to inspect the tree felling and pay the workers, he met two fishermen on the road loaded with fish. He told them to wait and, upon finishing his work, he would pick them up. When they reached town the passengers were afraid to get out of the car for fear that the soldiers would seize their catch. So, Father Cosmas drove them a further five kilometers beyond town and left them at the door of their huts.

On another occasion, when he was in Lubumbashi with his father, they drove, without stopping, past a man who was lying in the street. Suddenly, Father Cosmas stopped and turned back. "What's the matter?

Why are you going back?" his father asked. "That man is starving," he replied, "let's give him something to eat and help him back onto his feet." They picked him up trembling, and gave him a sizable amount of money so as to buy something to eat in a restaurant. Such scenes were repeated almost every day.

Whenever he wasn't loaded with material supplies, he would pick up people from the roadside. The poor people were often covering great distances on foot loaded down with their parcels of produce destined for sale in Kolwezi. He would often ask them to sing and derived great pleasure from listening to their beautiful voices.

Journeys on Swampy Roads

During the rainy season, which lasts six months, Father Cosmas avoided making journeys. But whenever there was an emergency, no danger or natural impediment was enough to daunt him. During this season flooded roads are often transformed into running streams and his vehicle would soon get bogged down in the mud. In such cases he would tie his car to a tree and, using a winch, pull it from the ditch and continue on his way. On other occasions, the road would be filled with deposits of silt and sand and the vehicle would become stuck. But the intrepid missionary had always his tools about him, including some special sheets of metal furnished with holes that allowed the wheels to engage and find some ground and so the car could get free of the sand.

Parish Feasts

During the eleven years that he spent in Zaire, Father Cosmas baptized some 15,000 Africans and founded nearly fifty-five parishes. At the feast commemorating the patron Saint of each parish, he used to donate two sacks of corn flour (for the making of *"bukari"* which is the African equivalent of bread) and a whole pig. Whenever he could he would attend the feast in person. He would bless the food and share in the eating of the *bukari*, to the joy of the Africans who were delighted to see a European partaking of their meal.

Flee From the Magicians

One of his earliest catechists, Nicodemos, remembering his former way of life, had gone to consult a magician. But the All-good God, who desires the salvation of all, allowed the catechist to be possessed by a demon. He remained like this for two days, so teaching his brethren what it means to return to one's former way of life and also how much the power of God surpasses the power of darkness. Father Cosmas read the prayer of exorcism over him and the demon came out of him.

The Authorities' Respect for Father Cosmas

Blessed Father Cosmas was the only missionary in Kolwezi who opened his arms to everyone. He even enjoyed good relations with the Local State authorities. Thus every Pascha or Christmas he used to present them with a pig from his farm as a gift, both enabling them to celebrate joyfully the feast days and Father Cosmas to gain their love and concern, all to the up-building of the mission. Thus, each time he or the Christians in general were faced with some difficulty, Father Cosmas had the understanding and cooperation of the competent officials.

Translation Work at the Mission Center

When Father Cosmas left his monastery at the age of 37 to travel to Kolwezi, he had not thought about the difficulties he might encounter. God had concealed the difficulties from him and had flooded his heart with love for his non-Christian brethren, and he was burning with zeal to reach them with the Gospel. He quickly realized that without knowledge of the language, ecclesiastical books, schools, dispensaries, pharmacies and churches he would achieve little.

He immediately took his pad of paper and wrote down a phrase in Swahili: "What is that?" and beginning with that phrase he embarked on a study of African languages, and of Swahili in particular. Asking the Africans a number of questions each day and writing down their replies in his notepad, he was able, after only a few months, to start speaking the language reasonably well. He advanced in learning and, with the help of the local Christians, soon commenced with the translation of ecclesiastical books.

He translated the services of Vespers, Matins, Compline, the rite of preparation before Holy Communion, Great Compline, the Paschal Service, the Lesser Blessing of the Waters (Agiasmos), the Funeral service, the Baptism and Marriage services, the Great Canon of St. Andrew of Crete and the Liturgy of the Presanctified Gifts, along with a variety of other liturgical hymns.

The Monastery of Simonopetra on Mount Athos likewise secured valuable help for the education of indigenous clergy through the involvement of Father Timothy (Hieromonk), who is from Zimbabwe and knows Swahili. He edited, in Swahili, sermons for the feast days of the Lord, of the Mother of God and of the Saints and sent the collection to the Mission in Kolwezi.

The work of translation has been continued by Father Cosmas' successors, who, to date, have produced the following editions: the Divine Liturgy in Greek and in a local dialect of Swahili, the Holy Gospel and the Book of Epistles, the Paraklitiki of all the eight tones, and the

Synaxarion of all the Saints of the year, containing their names, the way and year that they were martyred or reposed. The Liturgy of St. Basil was also translated from French and the Services for Holy Week are currently under preparation. The Triodion, Pentecostarion and, God willing, the *Menaia* are to follow.

The Pilgrimage Site and Oil Lamp of Father Cosmas

On the site of Father Cosmas' accident, which plunged not only Zaire's Orthodox into grief but also a large number of members of the civil and military authorities, the Orthodox Mission erected a small circular icon-stand made of metal in which an oil lamp burns before the icon of the Mother of God. It is probably the only shrine of its type in Zaire, and it proved difficult to obtain permission for it from the authorities concerned. For all the Orthodox faithful of Southern Zaire, this site will forever remain a stopping place where they will pause to pray, make the sign of the Cross, and discuss the burning apostolic figure of their Enlightener and Spiritual Father, Cosmas.

The person in charge of lighting this lamp each evening is the catechist who has begun a new parish for the Church in this area, the parish of St. James, and all the villagers are catechumens of the Orthodox Church. For every passerby the lit oil lamp is a mystery. They are all curious to know why there is a light burning there and what it represents. Little by little they all learn from the locals the way in which Orthodox honour and respect those who have sacrificed their life for the salvation of others; it has become a witness of their mission.

The Schools Run by the Orthodox Mission

For over ten years Father Cosmas worked hard to create the various projects of the Mission and before his sudden death he had laid the foundation of the "Light of Christ" primary school. Perhaps many people in Greece wonder what reason there is for the Mission to found schools. From the ecclesiastical side of things, what benefit are these schools to the Church, given that the lessons are taught according to the curriculum laid down by the State and, indeed, to children from the different Christian confessions? We are able to answer this question honestly and directly, since we have lived in Africa for years and are well acquainted with the present situation.

The Orthodox Mission appeared for the first time in 1972. Prior to this date, other priests had served the Greek community while simultaneously spreading the faith to the natives; before 1972-73, however, there were no missionaries whose sole task was the evangelization of the Africans of Zaire.

Before the arrival of the Orthodox, Roman Catholics had already been at work as colonizers and missionaries. They zealously built schools, hospitals, dispensaries and other community centers. During 130 years of labor they organized and divided Zaire into fifty dioceses. The Protestant groups, for their part, began their work in the 1920s and they have worked with the same zeal. It made an impression on us how much religious influence all the other missionaries have had on the Africans, primarily through education and the provision of medical care and subsequently through their religious work alone.

The Orthodox Mission encountered similar circumstances. The Africans first sought the foundation of schools and pharmacies and afterwards preaching, catechism and the building of churches. The situation, however, for the Orthodox was still more acutely problematic since Orthodox children are refused entry into schools of other denominations, and worse still, are even forbidden to play in front of the gates of other schools.

It was for this reason that Father Cosmas founded the "Light of Christ" primary school. This school began functioning in the 1990-91 school

Graduation ceremony at the Light of Christ School.

year, attended by 250 boys. Because of the school's expenses, priority was given to Orthodox children, and the remaining places were filled by other children.

To guarantee some sort of educational continuity, Father Cosmas' successor has also founded a secondary school at the instigation of Orthodox parents and in response to the justified demands of our faithful.

As for the country's schools in general, it is true to say that children in the villages stand in great need of some sort of education. Where there are many Christians, the people build schools for themselves out of brick and thatched roofing, using railway sleepers or knotted planks for benches. They pay for the teachers themselves out of their meager salaries, and ask from the Mission administrative oversight and a supply of stationery. When the widespread looting took place in September 1991, the Zairian government halted pay for teachers in State schools for lack of funds. Since then parents have sometimes been going even

Class in session at a school in one of the villages.

without their daily bread in order to be able to pay these teachers for their children's education.

The Orthodox Mission, for her part, pays teachers out of the money donated by the Churches of Kilkis and Giannitsa in Greece, thereby not having to require the children to pay tuition, something which does not happen with the other missionary groups. Children have only to pay an inscription fee, which is put towards buying stationery and repairing school buildings. In this way, in Zaire we provide, as far as possible, a free education: the fruit of Christian solidarity and of the Greek cultural tradition.

For six years the running of the primary was in the hands of Mrs. Efterpia Maftas-Ilias, a retired secondary school headmistress from Piraeus in Greece. Thanks to her fervent zeal, her experience in education and her sense of organization, she directed our schools so well that they became the models emulated by other educational establishments in Kolwezi.

Father Cosmas' Declaration After Death

Forty days after his death Father Cosmas appeared in a dream to Michael, a former catechist who now worked in the Mission's carpentry workshop, and said to him: "Michael, call Father Meletios and tell him to go to the place where I met my death. If he looks in the grass and dust there, he will find a flask of Holy Myrrh which I kept with me for baptisms, and my *epigonation* [the square piece of cloth worn at the side of a priest who is entitled to teach] along with a lance for the *Proskomidi*." Father Meletios and Michael, along with other of the brethren, went to the place and did indeed find these objects. The lance is now to be found in the Monastery of St. Gregory on the Holy Mountain.

Father Cosmas Demands the Return of the Flask

The day after Father Cosmas' accident, a Zairian from the area had gone to scour the accident site to see what he could find and evidently came across the Holy Myrrh. Believing it to be vegetable oil, he had taken it home with him to fry some fish. That night Father Cosmas appeared to him as he slept and told him in severe tones to return the flask to the place where he had found it or suffer a great misfortune. Sure enough some days later the man returned the flask to the place where Father Meletios was to find it.

Urged to Continue Catechism

While Father Cosmas was still living in this life, the group of catechumens included a certain army officer. After the unexpected death of his teacher, this man decided to stop attending catechism. Father Cosmas appeared to him one night and spoke to him kindly: "Why have you stopped your catechism? Go ahead with it and be baptized." But either out of indolence or because of his excessive grief he did not resume his catechism.

The Children at the Boarding School Told Us...

One day I had asked the children at the boarding school to tell me something exceptional about their spiritual father. They told me that one day as they were on their way to Compline and were passing by his grave they heard the peculiar sound of a censer. On other days they've heard the sound of bells near his grave.

Zairian Priests Told Us...

It was 28th August 1991, the last evening of our Theological Seminar and the last occasion that all the priests, catechists and teachers would pray Compline together. The priests were walking in front and the catechists behind, with the author of this book and certain other co-workers in the rear. As we came to the tomb of Father Cosmas the priests exclaimed in astonishment, "What are those lights?" They had seen with their own eyes luminous rays rising out of the tomb in a semicircular arc and extending beyond the height of the trees. I questioned three or four priests and all assured me that they had seen the same thing.

Fr. Cosmas' Intercession Heals the Sub-deacon Seraphim Ilunga

Seraphim Ilunga, a faithful believer and teacher at the secondary school in Kamina, told me the following: "Two years after the death of Father Cosmas, in 1991, I was ill. I spent a year away in Kaniama. One day he appeared to me and said: 'I know about your sickness and have come to heal you.' I thought I was inside of the Church of St. George in Kolwezi and then Father Cosmas called to me: 'Seraphim! Come outside.' He asked me to raise my shirt up. I did so and noticed uncleanness, like dirty water, issuing from my chest. I woke up and felt completely healthy again. I told my wife, Temelina, and other Christians what had happened and we all glorified God and His servant Fr. Cosmas for the boldness and glory that he found before Him. Since that day I have not suffered from any severe sickness."

On Father Cosmas' final visit to Lubumbashi he greeted Seraphim for the last time (who was a student in Lubumbashi at the time) and had given him 1,000 zaires. He used this money to buy the book *The Way of the Pilgrim* in French. Together with the others, they served Fr. Cosmas' final Liturgy in the beautiful temple of the Annunciation of the Theotokos.

Seraphim went on to say: "His meek face made a great impression on me that day. In his homily he spoke about repentance, eyes full of tears. When I learnt of his death, I wept. Not long thereafter, in February of 1989, I saw Fr. Cosmas in a dream and asked him: 'Father Cosmas, are you dead?' 'No, not dead, but resurrected. Look in my tomb, am I not resurrected?' Then, I saw in my sleep that he had opened his tomb and he was resurrected."

Seraphim also said to me: "In August 1989 my wife gave birth to a boy. Forty days later, as I was wondering what name to give to my child, Father Cosmas came to me in the middle of the night in my sleep and said: 'He should bear the name of Cosmas Aitolos.' "

Incidents and Accounts of Witchcraft

"He is Greater than Me"

While Father Cosmas was still in this world, he had come to our monastery one time on retreat and he related to me the following incident: in a certain village which is home to one of our Orthodox parishes, he had succeeded, thanks to the backing of the commissioner for Kolwezi, in having one of our faithful elected to the post of village chief. It is a fact that all over Africa numerous people practice sorcery whatever their social status may happen to be. Each village chief is the main person responsible within his jurisdiction for all matters relating to the life and well-being of the inhabitants: he is in charge of administration, medical care, schools and all ethnic, religious or moral affairs. The result is that all the villagers turn to him for help in any area, including religion.

This Orthodox believer, then, who had been elected village chief, had encountered some problem and remembered the sorcerer-in-chief in the large neighboring village, and went to visit him to ask for help. The witch doctor responded memorably: "I am unable to help you because there is another sorcerer whose power is greater than mine, and I mean the one who baptized you [he was referring to Blessed Father Cosmas]. I cannot act against him; I cannot even come near him. Go to him for help, he is greater than me!" Such was the sorcerer's open admission.

The Vicious Circle of Demonocracy

"... At the time we were touring the villages and, before we entered the city of Likashi, at a distance of about 15 kilometers, we stopped with two other cars in the middle of the road, which had been closed on account of the multitude of people.

"More than five hundred people were running up and down the road terrified. Then, a few minutes later, there appeared before me four natives, with burning cheeks and drenched with sweat, carrying on their shoulders a child's coffin. The crowd followed behind them, screaming and full of fear. They were heading in our direction with a quick and steady pace. Suddenly, an unseen power drove them all sideways and to the right. In this way they were removed from the road that led to the cemetery. As they insisted on continuing, it took them around in circles two or three times at a high velocity. The most important aspect of it all was that the coffin appeared as if it was nailed to their shoulders. Finally, they were turned toward the houses and then again into the ravine and onto the road, etc. I asked three different people at three different spots and all three answered me fearfully: "Father, magic is behind it all."

"I ask our aged driver for a more detailed explanation and he also answered me full of fear: "Father, from the time I was a young boy I heard about this kind of witchcraft but never believed it. But now I see it and it is true. The father of the boy went to the witch doctor and asked him to do his magic so as to reveal who it was that did witchcraft and killed his son. Now the dead boy (that's what the native driver maintained) won't allow them to transport his body to the cemetery until he leads them to the person who caused him to die. When the cause is punished, that is, dies, then the people will be free to take the deceased to his grave."

"Fine," I told him, "but why don't those who are being tormented by carrying the coffin on their backs, and being led left and right, put the coffin down?" He told me: "They can't. It's as if the coffin is stuck to their shoulders. But, in addition to this, they also want to help the father find the cause of his son's death. In another case, they set the coffin down and it moved on its own until it arrived at the house of the person who had done the witchcraft." Then I told him: "Those people will die from exhaustion, and to what end? I will read a prayer for the deceased

The Vicious Circle of Demonocracy

Great Friday; censing the Holy Crucified One.

so that Satan will leave them in peace to bury him." "No," one of the catechumens says to me. "If you read the prayer, Father, the witchcraft will come to an end, but later the father and his relatives will come and attack us, since they have paid the witch doctor to reveal, by means of magic, the person who did the witchcraft and killed the child."

"So, I was found in a dead end. A vicious circle of demonocracy. The crowd became wilder from its fear, so as soon as the road opened we left.

"We continued our journey; however, as we were leaving the village I observed the terrified people running like a herd with the agonizing question: Who among them will be the victim of the black magic?

"After a few days we passed by the village again. I wanted to learn the results of the case, for I had seen with my own eyes the power of Satan—how he had spun the whole village around. Still, I said to myself that it could all be a clever masquerade. The outcome was the following: The coffin, after taking many paths, flew in the air straight-ahead, as they told me, and pounded into the head of a woman, who immediately fell dead. Everyone considered her to be the cause of the child's death. This was also certified by the witch doctor. Thus, in this way, the witchcraft of the magicians turned out two victims. The bodies remained one on top of the other for three days until finally, by intervention of the military, they were transported to the cemetery.

"It should be noted that many state officials or magistrates, when cases arrive in their hands, overtly convict the witch doctor. After a little while, however, out of fear that maybe the sorcerer will work his witchcraft on them, they set them free, and thus the reign and rule of the witch doctors in Africa continues.

"The day before yesterday, Palm Sunday, I was in Likashi when we found a twelve year old boy, dead, in the grass about 200 meters from the church. They had used a syringe to extract all his blood for use in various acts of sorcery.

"It is common in the same way to find corpses with the heart taken out for sorcerers to perform their evil practices. This happens above all with small children. They are captured and taken out into the forest and have their hearts torn out even while still alive.

"A priest, Father Romanos, visited a woman in jail who told him that she had travelled from Kananga to Lubumbashi with her aeroplane at night and crashed in Fungurume, as she had run out of gas. Her aeroplane was a stalk of corn with two wings of a hen on the right and left. It was made by a magician and the gas was the blood of a baby, which the witch doctor inserts within the heart of the stalk with a syringe. Immediately, it began to work and fly in the air, transporting its passenger. The flying always happens in the middle of the night and for evil intentions.

"It is a fact, dear brother, that witchcraft is something with real consequences. In this way, all the Africans lived under the fear of magic. Until this day I have not found even one local Christian who does not fear the witch doctor...

Deceived by the Love of Money

The story, which we are about to relate, is a terrible one. It reveals the power of Satan and teaches us by the same token the greatness of Orthodoxy and the spiritual power of the successors of Christ, our Orthodox priests.

Father Photios from Fungurume told us how his son had been trapped in the snares of magic because he wanted to grow rich effortlessly. He is Orthodox and his name is Berde (in the beginning they were baptized here preserving their old name, by dictate of the state). He is married and works in the village of Kando, 50 kilometers from Kolwezi, where he sells different sorts of drinks.

One day a magician con artist arrived in the village. When he saw how well-kept Berde's house was, he asked for permission to go in and said: "I can bring in customers who will help you earn a lot of money in a short time." He immediately began performing his conjuring tricks in front of a large number of people. He took a piece of paper which he had first put in his mouth, spat on it, rubbed it and the paper was transformed into a snake. Then this snake became a piece of paper again which subsequently turned into other objects and animals. The spectators watching this performance were all in amazement and believed they had a "god" in front of them.

Our young Berde said to him: "I am an Orthodox Christian and I do not know if what you are proposing to me is of God or of the Devil. I will ask my wife first and then give you an answer." His wife said to him that the business of selling drinks had been tried already and didn't go well. Her husband disagreed and told her that he was heavy at heart, but in the end he yielded to the pressure of his wife who was not Orthodox. "Let us buy some magic concoctions," she told him, "and you'll see what joy will come to our house."

So they asked the magician to help them. He took two bottles of water and tossed his potions inside and the water turned an orange color. He covered one of the bottles with a woman's handkerchief and went and buried it in the courtyard, and he said to the married couple: "That bottle stands for a dead woman from the past who is going to attract people to buy beer in your bar." In the other bottle he placed a photograph of Berde and burrowed a hole behind a door in the house in which to bury the bottle. The sorcerer went on to make a little scratch in each of the couple's right hands and smeared it with a magic substance, the rest of which he threw onto the roof of the house. He then took four tree branches and placed them in the four corners of the house. Finally he told them: "With these branches and the powder on your roof another magician will be unable to enter your house, and even lightning will be prevented from striking it. And from now on many customers will come to your store and you will make a lot of money." Berde asked what he owed him in return, and he replied that he wanted to be paid in money.

"How much?"

"I will stay with you for three days and you must give me what I ask for when I leave," was the sorcerer's reply.

Berde made 500,000 zaires on the first day, and the same amount on the following days, so that after three days he had made 1,500,000 zaires.

The sorcerer then said to him: "I am leaving, give me all your earnings from the last three days." He took the money and before leaving said to him: "Be very careful. Sleep with no woman other than your wife, and be sure to touch no dead bodies. Even should your brother die, you must not touch him. Steer well clear of corpses." With these words he took the money and left. Berde awaited customers as the days passed, but in vain. No one came to the bar. Gloom descended on the house now that nothing was going right and they hardly had even enough to eat.

One day he went to his field and gathered a bagful of manioc, a local produce, to take to Kolwezi to sell. With the money he made from selling the manioc he bought a sack of corn. That night, succumbing to the temptation of the Devil, he assaulted a woman and lay with her. He then drank *lutuku* (a strong local alcoholic brew) and became very drunk, and went on to eat a *diamba* plant (hashish), which made him lose his mind. He went mad and was no longer aware what he was doing. He spent the nights in the yards of strangers, soldiers would beat him and children would throw dirt at him as he roamed about the streets of Kolwezi crying, shouting, and disturbing everyone. He turned up at the Catholic Mission but was thrown out with a beating.

His father, Father Photios, was informed about his son's madness and wanderings in Kolwezi, and came to tell us the unhappy tale at the Orthodox Mission, sending three of his sons out to catch Berde and tie him up and bring him home to the village of Kisote.

When he arrived home, still bound, Berde said to his father: "Dad, when my brothers caught me, I saw a brilliant light like a flash of lightning. I do not think I will die." Father Photios asked him how he came to be in such a state and his son revealed the whole story. He was taken to the church, confessed, and as soon as the prayer of exorcism of St. Basil was read, the unclean spirit fled out of him and Berde left the church in a state of complete calm. He said to his father: "Let's go home and remove the magic substances that the sorcerer left."

Father Photios obtained the blessing of the priest in charge of the Mission and left for Kando with his son. When they arrived, Father Photios read the Service of the Lesser Blessing of Waters (*Agiasmos*) and removed the bottles and the tree branches, and, last of all, blessed the house and consecrated it with the sign of the Cross. He removed the photo of his son from one of the bottles and the handkerchief from on top of the other, made the sign of the Cross over the magic solutions and poured them on the ground.

As Father Photios was pouring out the contents of the bottle containing the concoctions, hoarse cries of some ghastly sort made themselves heard. He sprinkled the entire house with holy water as well as the places where the charms had been laid, and finally his son drank some too. His son went on to confess to him: "I wanted to work in obedience to God's will, but the Devil deceived me. I will not fall into the same trap again. I will remain faithful to our Church."

Having accomplished this apostolic ministry, Father Photios returned peacefully to the Mission and we glorified God when he told us the story. Nowadays, wherever he goes he is able to testify to the greatness of God by telling of the episode and so confirming the faith of Christians in his seven parishes.

The Orthodox Priest is a Fire to the Sorcerer

I have been a priest at the Orthodox Mission in Kolwezi for nearly ten years. I currently serve at the parishes of St. Andrew, St. Thomas, and St. Paraskevi. The story that I am about to tell occurred in the month of August, 1990, in the town of Kolwezi.

Father Meletios, who is in charge of our Mission, had received a request from two Christian families to visit them in order to resolve a problem involving sorcery. The priest in charge decided to send me, inasmuch as I was Zairian and better understood my fellow countrymen's problems.

A thirteen year-old boy from the Luba-Shaba tribe had been a sorcerer ever since the age of 7. It was his grandfather who had initiated him into the realms of black magic. This boy lived with his paternal uncle as his parents had thrown him out of the family home. An Orthodox family lived right next door to the boy's uncle.

In the quarter where this child sorcerer lived a sorceress discovered him and said to him: "You are to be my husband and guide on the path of sorcery." One day this sorceress sent the child out with instructions to "go in search of food", i.e. to find a victim to kill for the Christmas and New Year (Jan. 1st) feasts. By way of "food" the child sorcerer had found his uncle at home and secretly stole an item of underclothing, which he took to the sorceress. He then went to the house of the Orthodox Christians and gave an eggplant to one child and a fish to the other. The two children ate the food because they were hungry, but experienced a strange taste and thought that they were eating raw human flesh. When the first of the children had eaten what appeared to be eggplant, he lost his mind straight away.

The uncle of this boy sorcerer is a member of a Protestant religious community called Basantu. One day, as the pastor of this community was saying the prayers, he turned toward the uncle of the child and said in front of all his followers: "Your family is not well. In your house you have a boy who is a sorcerer. The boy's uncle then took his nephew to their "church." There they began to pray and the child drew a string with three knots in it from his mouth. He intended to kill three people by means of this string. The pastor asked the child sorcerer what the string signified, and he replied that one of the knots was for his uncle and that the other two were for the two children of a certain family. The boy then said: "Let's go to the house of these Orthodox Christians." They asked to be allowed to go in. In each of the rooms where the children slept, there was a thick root planted beneath the bed which they tore up, since it was intended to exert a fatal Satanic influence on the children when they lay down to sleep at night.

The parents of the Orthodox family had thought it right in the meantime to summon an Orthodox priest. And so it came about that at Father Meletios' request I went to see them. I called for the child sorcerer and we sat down to talk. First of all I asked his uncle: "Do you know about your nephew's problem?"

"Yes, I'm aware that he is a sorcerer," he said.

And I asked the child too: "Are you a sorcerer?"

"Yes, I am."

"Hand over to me all your sorcerer's equipment."

The child replied: "I can't because there is a woman who will be angry and kill me."

I said to him: "No, she will not; if you believe in the true God you will not be killed." His hands were bound, so I undid them and said: "Our God loves you and will help you."

The child replied: "We perform our rites in the cemetery at the dead of night."

"How did you begin, and how do you recruit others to your evil practices?"

"We take the underclothes or the thread of a garment belonging to the person we want to cast a spell on, to kill or to recruit to our group."

"So if you touch somebody's clothing you're able to cast a spell on them; is that what you are saying?"

"Yes, it is very easy."

"So if you took a thread or touched my garment you would be able to spellbind me?"

"No! Not you! There is a fire surrounding you which will burn me if I come near."

I then addressed his parents: "Is your child a sorcerer?"

"Yes, he has been since the age of seven."

"We must help him to escape from sorcery or else his life will be nothing but trouble. If today he goes into an Orthodox Christian house, tomorrow it will be somewhere else and the day after he will be in prison. And you will have to pay the State a fine and compensation to the people to whom he has caused harm."

Lastly, I called together all the Orthodox Christians in the area, took a list of their names and performed the Office of the Lesser Blessing of the Waters (*Agiasmos*) followed by a reading of St. Basil's prayers of exorcism. I then anointed the two children with myrrh from the Mother of God of Malevi, given to me by the Fathers at the Mission. Everybody was glad and gave glory to God. Since then the children have been caused no problems by demons. They attend church, confess and take communion. It should be noted that as soon as he returned home, the child sorcerer completely lost his mind.

Powerless Before the Power of God

One other time Father James had gone to his village, Lualaba. There he had met an old friend who had become a sorcerer. They talked together about God and Father James proposed that the sorcerer come to church to see how evening prayer (Vespers) was conducted. His friend came to our church and watched everything carefully from a distance. At the end the sorcerer said to his old friend: "As far as I have been able to see, we both worship one and the same God. You cense your altar as I do, you offer up prayers and I do. There is no difference."

Father James replied: "All right then, let's go to your 'church' next." But the other flatly refused saying: "No, don't come, I can't pray if you are present. Even before, when you used to say that you would pray for me from a distance, I was left powerless. How much more likely is that to be the case if you come to my house!"

One can conclude from this story that the servants of Satan find themselves totally disarmed before the power of God.

The Decisive Blow

Whenever possible the Church performs the baptisms of catechumens in the villages during the dry season from May to October. So it was that Father Meletios had gone to baptize the catechumens in Fungurume, and had then gone on to the village of Tenke. As Father was performing the exorcism before baptism, a young girl fell to the ground unconscious. The spirit of Satan wanted to torture her, for she had left his worship and entered into the faith of our Orthodox Church, which is so brilliantly filled with light. A moment later she came to and was baptized along with the others, and thus dealt the decisive blow to the beast of this present age.

A Young Sorcerer Comes to the Light

During the month of September, 1994, we left Kolwezi to perform some baptisms in the villages of Kasaji, nearly 350km from Kolwezi. Our first stop was in Mwenye-Kula at St. Catherine's Orthodox Church. I would like to draw attention here to an incident that moved me.

In the evening all the catechumens came for confession. Among them was a sixteen year-old boy who came to surrender his magic items to Father Cosmas of Kawayongo. On the following day, full of joy and resolve, he came to Christ and was baptized, taking the name of Augustine. The cult of darkness in his life was finished. "All is filled with light!"

The Refusal to Surrender His Magic Objects

Father Romanos told me of the following incident that occurred in the Fungurume parish of St. John the Theologian:

"In 1985 I was the priest at the Saint John the Theologian parish in Fungurume. One Sunday the blessed Father Cosmas came to do baptisms. After his last counsels and strict recommendations to the catechumens, he stressed: "For those who have occupied themselves with witchcraft in the past, bring me all the objects and potions that you were using, sometime before this evening." Quite a few people brought to him wooden idols, liquids, snake-skins and other such things. One of the catechumens, whose name was Sabachila, didn't bring his paraphernalia to Father Cosmas. He was baptized the next day without turning in his objects and without confessing the matter.

He passed about seven months without going to church at all on Sundays. One Sunday he decided to go, carrying with him in his pocket his own little "god," a wooden idol, which for him was his god, his hope, his guardian and his refuge in every event of evil. Indeed, before entering the church he held within himself the following strange thought: "Now we will see what power the Orthodox Church possesses, which says that it is stronger and greater than the magicians and their witchcraft."

When he entered and went up to venerate the icon of St. John the Theologian, as he had been taught months before in catechism, he felt something like electricity spread throughout his body. Strong pain had extended everywhere and he kept silent with a sense of agony as to what would happen to him. The others knew nothing of his condition. At the end of Liturgy everyone departed, the young magician included, who arrived home filled with staggering pains throughout his body.

After a few days his pain increased. His condition grew worse and he was taken to the Jecamine hospital in Kakanda. The doctors, despite their noble efforts, were not able to relieve him from his pain definitively. He returned home devoid of hope. After four days he came to church. He entered in and said to me: "Father Romanos, I am going to die. My illness originated with the icon of Saint John the Theologian. When I venerated it a few months ago something like electricity spread throughout my body."

I said to him: "I have nothing of my own to tell you. Go and venerate the icon of Saint John the Theologian again, this time with repentance and you will be healed." He told me: "If I look at this icon of Saint John in the eyes, I'll die." He didn't venerate the icon, returning to his house sick as before.

After a little while Father Cosmas visited the newly-illumined of Fungurume. He met with Sabachila, who recounted to him his whole saga. Father counseled him to venerate the Saint, but he refused once again, saying that he would die if he venerated the Saint's icon. The Greek doctor Thanos Tzotzos also advised him the same, but the magician "understood not" (Acts 7:24).

His end was not long in coming. In a few days he died amidst horrific pain, captive to Satan and scorner of the Holy and Orthodox Baptism.

The Sad Departure of a Roman Catholic Missionary

Father Joseph from Lubumbashi told us of a phenomenal and tragic incident, which happened in Kinshasa, the capital of Congo.

When he was living in the capital, which was also his birthplace, there occurred an incident at a church of the Roman Catholics. At that time he and his parents and sisters and brothers were all Roman Catholics.

The one responsible for this church was a priest who had come from Belgium to work in the mission field of Zaire. With his personal zeal he had managed to lead many Africans into his church. Across the street from his church, however, a witch doctor had set up his "headquarters." Each evening, at the very same time that the Roman Catholic priest held his services, the sorcerer sounded his bongo, gathered people around and performed his magic ceremonies. He would lay out his wooden idols to dance, the people would sing and, in general, create a lot of noise and commotion and upset the commendable efforts of the Roman Catholic priest.

He suggested another time for the magician to call his followers, but he would hear nothing of it. He asked them not to make so much noise, but once again they were unmoved.

Thus, the priest was forced one day to go to the demonic gathering in person. Somewhat angry and irritated, he grabbed for the wooden idols in order to toss them in the trash. But what befell the hapless one! One of the larger of the idols stuck to his palm and wouldn't detach for anything. The priest tugged at it desperately, but all in vain. His rage reached its peak. Then the magician said to him: "If you leave me alone to do my work, then neither will my objects be of trouble to you." The Roman Catholic priest promised him that he would not concern himself with the magician's work again. Thus, at the command of the sorcerer the idols were loosed from his hands. The priest from shame and resentment departed forever for his homeland of Belgium with the first available flight.

A Protestant Missionary Receives a Teaching

In the month of August, 1994, all Kolwezi was in a state of commotion over advertisements, posters and placards throughout the town announcing that "Christ" would be coming to heal the sick and infirm, the blind and the lame of the whole area. Thousands of dollars had been spent preparing

A Protestant Missionary Receives a Teaching

Young chanters, come to Kolwezi for the annual summer seminar, gathered around Father Meletios at the church of St. George.

for the reception of a Pentecostal minister who was coming from South Africa to heal the sick of Zaire.

The same welcome and festivities awaited him in Lubumbashi where many sick people had followed him in the hope of being healed. The start of this new "messiah's" preaching and healing coincided with the start of the services of the Supplications to the Mother of God, which the Orthodox celebrate during the month of August. Our Rev. Father, Archimandrite Meletios, had given Orthodox Christians advance warning of the arrival of this pseudo-messiah and had forbidden our faithful to go to his meetings even out of curiosity. He had given permission only for two or three Christians to go and listen to what he had to say so as to be able to inform those in charge of the Orthodox Mission.

Each evening the "messiah" would call out to the people in English and two people would translate his words into French and Swahili in thunderous tones so that people would come up en masse to be healed. At the same time Father Meletios was in our church of St. George, barely one hundred meters from the demonic assembly, praying the Supplications to the Mother of God, as well as the prayer-rope on bended knee, along with preaching and homilies. The two assemblies were competing to see who would prevail.

The result was made clear the next day, Sunday evening, from the very lips of this presumptuous Pentecostal preacher and performer of false miracles. "I have been to numerous cities and countries, and everywhere my preaching has met with success, but what I underwent here in Kolwezi has happened to me for the first time. I have been here for so many days and yet have not managed to perform a single healing. I ask myself why? I think there is some other force present here in your city, beloved, which, strangely enough, doesn't allow me to 'heal' you and bring you all to believe in Jesus Christ. I am leaving feeling very embittered and will not be able to return to your city."

This miracle of Christ and of the Mother of God was thus confirmed by the very confession of the enemy of Truth. The news was passed on to our faithful on the following Sunday, and they gave glory to God and celebrated the outcome with hymns and chants.

Miracles, Missionary Work and Signs from the Saints

We want the Apolytikion of St. Patapios[36]

One evening a pious Zairian couple arrived at our Mission Center. I knew them very well because they are assiduous followers of our liturgical Services and of our catechetical teaching. They said to me: "Father, will you give us the *Apolytikion* and the *Kontakion* of St. Patapios?"

"Why is that? And how do you know about St. Patapios?" I asked.

The husband replied as follows: "Recently we have been through a lot of difficulties in our house. We prayed hard at night for God's help. One night I had this vision in a dream. I could see that I was holding tightly onto a rope and walking towards one of our churches without touching the ground, and my wife was walking behind me in exactly the same way. At that moment, a monk came out of the church and said to us: 'Do not be downcast about your problems. Take this Gospel and this prayer-rope, read, pray and call upon my name and I will help you. I am St. Patapios.' "

They felt that they received these gifts from his hands, and that the Bible was open at the Gospel of St. John. To be sure, with the help of a Zairian, I translated the chants in honour of St. Patapios into Swahili and gave them to the couple, with an icon of the saint.

---

36 St. Patapios died towards the end of the sixth century and his body was found in a grotto in the Peloponnese in 1911. His feast day is December 8th.

Priests of the Orthodox Church in Zaire.

Go to the True Church where the Priests have Beards and Cassocks

One morning in May, 1994, a middle-aged Zairian arrived at our Mission. I welcomed him and he told me his problem. He seemed troubled and uneasy and said the following: "Father, I am a worker at Jecamine. I fell seriously ill. As the doctors were unable to help me, I asked God to have mercy on me." I asked him to which church he belonged.

"I am a Roman Catholic," he replied. "One night I saw in a dream several priests like yourself wearing brilliant vestments and celebrating the Liturgy in a church like yours. One of the priests approached me and said: 'God has heard your prayer, but for your salvation you must join our Church, for it is the only true Church.' I do not know you or the name of your Church, but I have approached you because in my dream

I saw priests like you, with beards, cassocks and brilliant vestments. I asked other people who told me that only Orthodox priests have beards and wear cassocks and other such clothing, and they also told me where to find your church."

I advised him and gave him a book, and suggested that he come to our church for catechism every Sunday. Since then he has been a faithful member of our church, and has not perished from the grave illness, which so afflicted him.

A Roman Catholic is Led to the True Church

In the month of March, 1991, the priest in charge of the Orthodox Mission Center in Kolwezi, Archimandrite Meletios, had left for Likashi to celebrate the Forty Day Memorial service following the death of a Greek woman called Sophia. One evening, as he was walking along the street towards the church of St. John the Forerunner, he noticed that a Zairian woman was following him. She drew near him and asked his pardon, and then told him the following: "Father, I am a Roman Catholic. Every day I ask God for guidance towards salvation. One night I had a dream. I saw a priest dressed as you are, with a cassock and a beard, and his face seemed to be full of light. He came up to me and spoke to me in Swahili, which amazed me, as this was the first time I had seen him. He showed me a church and said: "Since you plead with tears to be shown salvation, behold, here is the true church where you will find it. Go to this church and the priest will tell you what you must do to be baptized."

Father Meletios listened to her with interest until they arrived at the church of St. John the Forerunner when the woman suddenly cried out: "This is the church that I saw in my dream!" She broke down in tears of joy and emotion.

The Dove and the Glimmering Flame

Among the clergy and members of our Mission in Kolwezi is a deacon named Lazarus. He stands out for his great obedience, humility and love of his work.

One day I went up to him and asked: "Father, how did you become Orthodox?"

"I remained unbaptised until 1983. I heard talk of the Methodists and I approached them to begin with. I followed their teaching, but when they proposed baptizing me I sensed that my soul was resistant to the idea. I then went to the Pentecostals, but I left them for the same reason. My soul could not find peace anywhere.

"One day as I passed the Orthodox Church my thoughts urged me to enter. I felt peace and inner joy. An inner voice told me that this was the True Church for which I had been searching. I asked to see the priest who at the time was Father Cosmas. I attended catechism and a year later was baptized with other brethren. As I emerged from the baptismal font I saw a dove hovering above the heads of the other newly-illumined brethren. The others saw the same thing as well. Father Cosmas explained that this was the symbol of the descent of the Holy Spirit upon us, just as He had descended at the Baptism of Christ in the Jordan."

"Father Lazarus, how did you become a deacon?"

"Father Cosmas proposed to Archbishop Timothy that I take up this lofty service. I remember the ordination well: as I bowed my head at the Holy Altar and the Bishop laid his hand on my head and read the prayer of ordination, a flame like a burning candle lit up within my heart. I experienced then such joy that I asked Christ never to let this fire be extinguished within me. But after a while the fire grew weaker. I begged God not to let it go out. An inner voice consoled me, telling me that there would always remain a spark. And it is this glimmering flame that I experience, sometimes weakening and other times intensifying."

"Your Faith Has Made You Well"

As we well know, it is by means of faith that a believer can receive the grace of God. God's mighty gift is beginning to become apparent to the young Orthodox believers of Zaire. The story that I am about to tell took place in the spring of 1994.

Deacon Lazarus' wife was suffering from high blood pressure. We were all afraid because her pressure had reached 28TA and to us it was a miracle that she was still alive. We took her to Lubumbashi to the "Don Bosco", a modern and well-equipped hospital belonging to the Roman Catholic Church. The doctors there examined her and with the help of treatment managed to reduce the pressure. The situation grew less anxious. But when we returned to Kolwezi her pressure was very high once again. It was now that Maria said to us: "I will go to the church of St. Nektarios next to the Mission's clinic and I will not leave there until he has cured me." The woman took a small icon of the saint in her hand, which she had asked for from her husband, and went and took up position standing and praying in front of the large icon of St. Nektarios in the church's icon screen. Her husband, Deacon Lazarus, was standing at her side with the same faith and conviction. They spent the whole night like this, praying. In the morning her health was completely restored. St. Nektarios had performed a miracle. Since that day the woman has been hard at work in the fields as before, without any health problems. Glory to God and his Saints for their miracles!

A Young Girl is Brought Back to Life

One evening in May, 1994, I had gone to the village of Musonoi about 4km away from Kolwezi. We have a parish there of the Ss. Theodore, with a beautiful church built by Father Cosmas. I met Simeon, our catechist, and discussed parish affairs with him. I asked him to tell me whether the two Saints Theodore help them or not. He replied: "Yes, they help us a lot, Father. Do you see that young girl over there? She had died and the Saints brought her back to life." While we were talking this little girl was busy playing with other girls in the churchyard.

"How was she brought back to life? I would like to hear the account," I said to him.

"It was one evening, she was playing outside the church with some other children. She felt thirsty from the hot weather, and left to go home. Outside the house, right next to it, stood a large 200-litre vat half-full of water. The child climbed on top of this vat and cupped her hands to drink from it, but lost her balance and fell into the vat, and was drowned. In the meantime the other children were waiting for her to come back, but she did not.

"Not long afterwards her mother arrived back from the fields. The other children told her that they had no idea where their friend was. So the mother set about looking for her child and began to cry. When she went to draw water from the vat, she found her child there, already dead. Her cries and wails were indescribable. "For my part," said Simeon, "I urged her to stay calm and to take the child into the church. If the saints so wish it, they could bring her back to life.

"The mother took the child and went to the church. When they reached the door of the church the child started vomiting water through its mouth. She opened her eyes and asked her mother "Where are we going?"

"God's Saints had performed their miracle. It is impossible to describe everyone's joy. On the following day we celebrated the Divine Liturgy and gave glory to the Saints for this miracle."

An Idol-worshipping Woman

The two Saints Theodore performed another miracle in the parish of Musonoi, this time in 1993. Simeon the catechist told us the details:

"In the spring of 1993, during the fighting between the Katanga and the Kasai tribes, there was a lot of trouble here in Musonoi and a large number of people were killed. A Kasai woman who was an idolater had a child who had been a long time sick with malaria. Her friends and parents were urging her to go to the witch doctor as quickly as possible before the child died. There was also the problem of how to get away from the area to go to central Zaire, which is her tribe's homeland, as the Katanga were driving the Kasai out and pillaging and burning their homes. The idolater said to her parents: "I have been told that there are Orthodox here and the people who dwell in their church perform miracles. I am going there." She was referring to the two Saints Theodore. Therefore, she took her child, who was on the verge of death, in her arms and went as fast as she could to the church of Ss. Theodore in Musonoi.

"As she approached the entrance to the church her child woke from its heavy sleep, in fine health, and asked to eat. The saints had performed their miracle. The woman went into the church, gave thanks to the two saints and made her joyful news known to everyone."

"Not This Way . . . There is a Church There"

At the time of the tribal fighting, another miraculous occurrence took place. A group of twenty-eight soldiers, with an officer at their head, had left Kolwezi and were making for the village of Musonoi. They belonged to the Katanga and intended to attack the Kasai. Among the intended victims were many Orthodox Christians from our parish of Ss. Theodore.

As the group of soldiers came running, machete blades in hand, down the road leading to our church, the leader was heard to say: "We can't go this way. There is a church there." They turned back and went round another way to resume their pursuit of the Kasai. The Ss. Theodore had performed yet another miracle and saved our Kasai Christians who lived next to their church.

One ought to note that on the same road before arriving at our church there are also two or three "churches" belonging to Protestant communities, and that the soldiers in question had swept through there unhindered leaving numerous victims in their trail.

A Boarding School Student told us…

At our Mission boarding-school there are a number of children, and one of them, Joseph from Musonoi who belongs to the parish of Ss. Theodore, told me the following miraculous story about the Saints of his church.

"When I was a small child," he said, "I suffered terrible stomach-aches. One night the two Saints Theodore appeared to me and said: "Don't worry. We will take care of you." In the morning all trace of my illness had completely disappeared.

"Another time I was playing with other children outside the church while the catechists and faithful were inside reading the Vespers service. I played outside, indifferent and without even the thought of going inside for Vespers. That night the Saints came to me in my sleep and told me: 'When there are services in church you should also go inside and pray, just as the other Christians do. If you carry on playing at those times we will discipline you'. I paid no attention to their words and continued playing as in the past.

The second time they visited me they said with strictness: 'Why did you not listen to our advice?' I didn't answer them and they began to strike me with a whip. In the morning when I woke up the whole of my body was hurting. But, because I was young and careless, I continued to play while church services were being held. I received a second violent reprimand from the Saints and only afterwards changed my behavior."

Theft at the Parish of Ss. Theodore

In 1982 some thieves broke into the church and stole icons, oil lamps and various other items. They discarded them out in the bush somewhere, and a year later some children discovered them as they were playing and called Father Cosmas who came to fetch them. They had not suffered any damage in spite of being exposed to the rain, heat, insects etc., for a whole year.

Spiritual Advice

The catechist of the parish of Ss. Theodore in Musonoi told me about the following incident:

"Since we suffer from the repeated break-ins of thieves Fr. Cosmas, in order to protect our parish, appointed one of our Christians as a night watchman. One night, as the watchman was making his rounds doing his duty, the protector of our parish, Saint Theodore the Commander, paid him a visit. 'Do not drink wine to get drunk, do not harbor ill feeling one against the other, do not commit adultery. Don't allow those who have not been baptized Orthodox to enter the church.' When Father Cosmas learned of this, he gave us as a blessing an icon of the Saint and told us to keep it in our house with much reverence and to call upon the Saint for help with all our problems."

Our Saints are with Us in All Circumstances

When our chanters sleep in the church at night they can hear the sound of horses coming into the church, entering the sanctuary and then vanishing. This happens especially on the night before and the night after the feast of Ss. Theodore each year. On the evening before, Christians and non-Christians alike can hear the chant of "Agios, Agios, Agios…" (Holy, Holy, Holy…). They ask our Orthodox parishioners: "What happens in your church during the night?" When a believer is praying in the church at night, he can often feel someone come and pat his shoulders. Every year on the commemorative feast day of Ss. Theodore there is abundant rain, a sign of blessing.

Healed by Saint Theodore

Among the catechumens that the catechist Simeon had in Musonoi, was a young girl who always had serious health problems. Simeon would go often to her house to console her and teach her the Word of God. They would often pray together or with the other catechumens of the parish of Ss. Theodore.

One day the child fell into a fit of vomiting that lasted more than thirty minutes. She became so weak as to appear dead. She fell asleep and saw one of the two Saints Theodore, who said to her: "Stand up, your illness is over." She stood up and felt better. She is now twenty-four years old. At baptism she took the name Agape. Since that time she has not visited a doctor or suffered any other illness.

Healed of Sterility

In the village of Musonoi, according to the testimony of the catechist and sub-deacon Simeon, the following incident occurred.

Women in the Congo, as is well known, give birth to many children and this is seen as a blessing of God. A particular woman had given birth to five children. Her desire was to have other children as well. Ten years passed by without a child. She drank syrup from herbs, consulted traditional healers and visited different doctors, but without any result. Finally she approached the Church and sought the intercession of the protectors of their parish, the two Saints Theodore. She conceived and bore a child who they named at baptism, Simeon, in honor of Saint Simeon the God-receiver as well as the sub-deacon and catechist who directed her to flee to the Saints for help.

The Child Should Die in Church

"One day," our catechist Elias told us, "my child was seriously ill. That night, at one o'clock in the morning, he showed various symptoms that told us, his parents, that he did not have long to live.

"I said to my wife, Catherine, that it is better that the child should die in church rather than in our house. We left the house and went together with the child to church. We kneeled before the icon of St. Demetrios. We begged him that the will of God and his be done. We also said the prayer 'Lord Jesus Christ heal our child through the prayers of the Great Martyr Demetrios' with the prayer-rope. We also anointed the child with oil from the icon lamp of St. Demetrios. And a little later we saw that, despite all the hopeless symptoms, the child's health was returning to him and that he was breathing normally again. From that time the child has not fallen ill again."

A Stroke of Lightning

Elias the catechist told me of another incident experienced by his parish of St. Demetrios. "In 1987 there were very heavy rainstorms, and lightning struck our church. We had seen bright flashes all over the village and heard tremendous claps of thunder. When I went that afternoon to the church, as usual, to celebrate Vespers, as I entered the sanctuary I found that the icon of Christ crucified had fallen down, the light in its oil lamp had gone out and the window had been broken. But the lightning had caused no other damage in the church."

An Outbreak of the Measles

Stavroula told us the following: "From 1980 until 1982 a measles epidemic descended upon our village. The sickness affected all of the small children, many of whom lost their lives. All of the Orthodox Christians gathered in our church, dedicated to the Great Martyr Anastasia, the Deliverer from Potions, and begged her to save our children. Although every day another two to five dead children from other families would be added to the total, not one of our children died. St. Anastasia lent miraculous protection to all our Orthodox children.

People asked themselves why it should be that Orthodox children did not die while other children were dying in numbers every day. From then on they considered us to be some kind of magicians and in vain did we try to explain to them that our Church is the True Church of Christ."

Miraculous Protection

Stavroula continued: "During the tribal and political tensions between the Katanga and the Kasai peoples, Saint Anastasia protected all the faithful from the attacks of the military who were looting the homes of a great many people and claiming numerous lives. Not one of the Christians from our village suffered loss of life or property."

Protected from Cholera

Our catechist, now sub-deacon, in the parish of the Twelve Apostles in Luena, Joachim, informed me of what had happened when the people of the village were all suffering from diarrhea and vomiting. At the time of the epidemic, a native priest, Fr. Iakovos, was with them and counseled them all to gather in the church, to pray and drink only holy water. One after another they all prayed using the prayer-rope, calling upon God to help, drinking some holy water and prostrating themselves before the icons of Christ, the Mother of God and all the Saints.

The disease did not affect a single member of our church, nor did any of them die from the epidemic. Everyone was amazed by this miracle of the Twelve Holy Apostles, and the Roman Catholics no less than the Protestants wondered why it should be that the Orthodox did not die.

"How Do You Orthodox Pray?"

The Deacon Achillas, who is from the town of Katanga, related to me the following account of a theft that took place in his house in 1994. He and his wife were absent from their house, working in the fields. Their oldest children had gone to school, while the three youngest were playing with other children outside in the yard. The burglar forced open a window and ransacked all three rooms, opening all the suitcases and scattering clothes all over the floor, taking a new coat and whatever money he found. When the deacon returned that evening he learned the news from the neighbors and found the house in a shambles. That night the deacon didn't go to sleep, as he told others, but together with his wife and other Christians he went to the Church of Saint Achillas and read the Supplications to the Holy Mother of God for her to reveal to them the thieves. She was not long in coming to his aid.

Three days later the piece of clothing was found in Bungubungu, some 5 kilometers from Katanga, where the thief had sold it. They found the thief and arrested him. As they were both from the same village, the deacon didn't want the state officials to punish him. As for the money, he returned half of it.

"That same month," continues Father Augustine Mwamba, "another burglary occurred, this time at the house of a catechist of the Roman Catholic Church. The couple had all their new clothes stolen. Having heard about the miracle, which had happened to our deacon, he came to ask how he should pray to God in order to recover his lost goods. The reply was that he should pray to the *Panagia* Virgin Mother of God with the prayer-rope. He returned home and did everything he could, with inquiries and investigations too, but all in vain. Everybody was amazed at how this miracle only held good for the Orthodox."

Seek First the Kingdom of God...and all These Things Shall be Added unto You

Father Augustine is the priest of the parish of St. John the Forerunner in Likashi. Together with his assistant, Fr. Paul, he serves alternately the eight villages that surround Likashi. Both priests are distinguished for their diligence and thoroughness in their pastoral duties. When one serves in Likashi the other will be found at one of the villages, and vice versa. They preserve between themselves brotherly love, respect, humility and a spirit of cooperation.

Father Augustine was blessed by God to have a large family, numbering thirteen children. The youngest has just turned one. The task of feeding and caring for them is great. Of course, the Mission Center in Kolwezi supports them by providing them with a salary, corn flour, and occasionally medicine and clothes. Their oldest children, after their school lessons finish, work on selling different small objects at the market, even including their own workbooks.

That, however, which especially moves us about the behavior of Father Augustine is that everyday he is always joyful. After the morning service he takes the hoe and his oldest children and walks a few kilometers into the forest where he readies the soil for seeding, turning and watering the ground that they might harvest their fruits in due season.

In those difficult moments, when the misery becomes tangible and encircles him, without grumbling and with unwavering faith he raises his hands high in order to ask for divine assistance. He is sure that he will not be turned away helpless and ashamed.

Many times he has told me about the different occasions in which Divine Providence has cared for his family. He has especial devotion to the Lady Theotokos, who, after his persistent prayer, saved his first grandchild, the son of his son. The baby was born premature and soon thereafter became sick and lost considerable weight. The women who had helped with his delivery placed the child in the egg incubation machine in lieu of an incubator in order to keep him warm. Father Augustine gave his Presbytera oil from the ever-lit oil lamp in the Church of Saint John the Forerunner and she anointed the child, mentally praying for the healing of her child. The next morning the baby began to move his hands. His weight increased and soon thereafter surpassed his birth weight by 400 grams. The miracle of faith had brought the desired result.

Another time, he was working the soil behind the church, as was usual after Matins. On that particular day they had nothing at home in the way of food! He called upon the Panagia at the hour of work: "O my Panagia, what will my children eat today? Please, I beg you to help us. Come and see that there is no food in our house."

That afternoon, strangely enough, a European suddenly arrived at the church. He asked for the priest, whom he had never met before. He gave him an envelope with money and told him: "Father, take that food for your family. Someone came to me in my sleep and told me to come here and give you this money. And whenever you have need, just come to my house and I will help you."

For all of this and more Father Augustine is full of joy, for he has learned to raise high his hands to heaven and call upon Divine Providence. May it be blessed that we too might acquire a little of his wonder-working faith.

Someone in a Cassock Enters the Church

In the parish of Saint John the Theologian in the village of Fungurume the parish priest is Father Photios and the sub-deacon, Panayiotis. Two years ago the latter related to me the following miraculous event that happened to his wife.

"My wife, Maria, suffered from severe stomach pains. Various Christians comforted her and counseled her to pray. She answered them thus: 'I pray to God but He does not hear me. I went into hospital but saw no improvement. I went to Father Photios and he told me to fast three days and pray without ceasing, but once again I found no remedy.'"

On the fourth day, after Vespers at seven o'clock, she stayed behind in church. She went and stood in front of the icon of the Lady Theotokos and said: "I ask you to help me just as you have helped other women. You can see that I am suffering a lot from my illness, dear Mother of God." Without feeling anything in particular she moved on to the icon of St. John the Theologian and prayed in the following manner: "You who are truly the divine Protector of this church, how is it that you defend us and yet I remain ill and you don't defend me nor heal me of my illness? Pray for me and intercede with God for Him to help me, sinner that I am, as there is nowhere else for me to turn for refuge. I have suffered greatly." With these words the poor soul began to cry with sobbing without, however, moving from her spot. She was intending to continue her prayers when someone suddenly opened the door of the church. It was someone in a cassock. With much piety and walking lightly he entered the Altar. He put incense in the censer and made ready to cense the temple. A fragrant smell spread throughout the church.

The woman was frightened and fled. She went and woke up her husband, to whom she told the whole story of this miraculous visit of St. John. He rebuked her for having run away. They went to report the incident to Father Photios who likewise chided her for having fled the church. She should have stayed to take the blessing of the Saint.

Afterwards they went all together to the church, where they could still smell the sweet fragrance from the visit of the Saint. From that evening onward the woman became well again and became firmly convinced that the Saints of our Church love us, help us and are near to us.

Saint David Walks in the Tent

Our catechist John, in the parish of Saint Athanasios in Musokatanda recounted the following:

"One Saturday afternoon, two of the brethren decided to go hunting out in the bush. I asked them, and finally admonished them, not to go, as in the evening we have the Service of Vespers and in the morning the Resurrection Service for Sunday. They didn't listen to me and left. Before they departed, I gave them a paper icon of Saint David the Elder of Euboia.

That night they arrived in the bush and laid down to rest a little before setting out to hunt later on. Soon thereafter one of them went a little ways off to relieve himself. In front of him, a few feet away, he saw a tall and lean monk walking by. It was Saint David of Euboia just as he appeared in the icon that they had been given by the catechist John. He ran to tell his companion, but when he had arrived the Saint had already departed. Alarmed by this sudden evening Visitor, they set out that same hour for the village. There they called upon the catechist and the other Christians and related the event. They came to the conclusion that they shouldn't be absent from the Church Services, for the Saints watch over them and want them to be in the church at the times of the Services and not out in the bush and fields.

A Miraculous Conversion

"One Saturday evening," I was told by our catechist Basil from Dilolo, "we were in our parish church of St. Anthony in Kambala saying the prayer of St. Cyprian.

"Outside, an unbelieving mother was walking past and heard the prayer. The next day, Sunday, she came to the church and asked to speak to the catechist for a moment. She was given permission and said: 'I had been sick for three months, with persistent bleeding. I went to the hospitals and witch doctors without success. I even turned to the churches belonging to other denominations but the illness did not stop. Today, however, I was healed simply by hearing the prayer of St. Cyprian in the Orthodox Church." After first being baptized, she and her husband were then married in the Church. Her husband is now the head of the parish assembly.

A Miraculous Intervention

John, the catechist in the parish of St. John Chrysostom in Kabundji, told me the following:

"In July of 1989 I attended the seminar for catechists at the Mission Center in Kolwezi. Upon returning home, I was very sick with a very bad case of diarrhea. My body's organism weakened terribly, and everyone in the village was sure that I would die. That night I saw in my sleep an Orthodox priest who resembled our Congolese priest, Father Agathonikos. He drew near me, took his *epitrachelion* (stole), laid it upon my head and read prayers for me. And then he told me: 'Don't worry. You'll be cured of your sickness.' He then left and by the time morning rolled around I was completely well."

A Miraculous Visit

John the catechist also told me about a Christian called Panteleimon who was ill. The catechist's wife had seen a priest who looked like Father Photios making for the sick man's house. John the catechist was out in the fields at the time, and on his return he was told that the priest had been to see Panteleimon and that if he wanted he could go and visit him. When he got to the sick man's house he asked if the priest had been to visit. The sick man replied that no, Father had not been but that at a given moment he had noticed a smell of incense burning and had felt a little better. A few days later he was completely better.

I saw the *Panagia* Theotokos

At the Monastery of St. Nektarios where we have our clinic and a boarding school for young girls, an 82-year old Greek grandmother was taken into medical care, Yiayia Christina. As she was left without help from relatives, she received the love and care of the Sisters of Saint Nektarios. Her legs were paralyzed and she remained practically immobile on her bed, praying to God the Jesus Prayer with her prayer-rope for all of us and lastly for herself.

In the autumn of 1994 she told us that she had seen the Mother of God: "I saw the *Panagia* Theotokos. I recognized her. It was she. Thousands of people were following her with lighted candles. She comforted me, blessed me and told me to walk." As she had lost her sight some twenty years earlier, she asked her companions to help her to stand up. She walked quite a bit, even venturing out into the garden. And although she remains in bed, she no longer feels any pain. This is what she told us herself.

She currently lives in Lubumbashi with her children. She is glad to receive many of her fellow brethren there and prays for everybody with her prayer rope as she awaits, without fear, the end of her life.

A New Saul Comes into the Church

The love of God is ingenious in the ways in which it visits with redemptive Grace the souls of men. It doesn't know distances, nor does it maintain preferences with respect to color, tribe, ethnicity, service or position in the world. Love, incarnate in the person of our Saviour Jesus Christ, wants to embrace, if possible, the entire race of men, but is obstructed by our self-love and individualism. However, where it meets a sincere struggle for salvation, where it finds raised hands and bended knees, it leaves the heavens and descends. The love of the Father is moved to carry out its intention in its own way, unknown to us.

Listen, brethren, to a story from the Mission field.

Not even Paul, the Apostle of the Nations, believed that on his way to Damascus he would meet the Lord whom he was persecuting. Nor did Saint Cyprian, in his attempts to be victorious over the faith and prudence of a young lady, Justina, expect to meet the living God. Only when included among these and other examples from our Church's history, does the present narrative not cause astonishment, inserted as it is in the long line of God's wondrous love of Man. I present it just as I heard from the new Saul himself, the native Tamboue.

One January morning in 1991, the native priest Father Iakovos entered the yard of the Mission Center with the young Zairian, Tamboue. They greeted me warmly and Father Iakovos said to me in front of the young man: "He wants to become Orthodox. I leave him to you to tell him what you think." Instead of bombarding him with questions, I asked the man to tell me his life's story and how he had arrived here. He was a lean, serious looking and self-collected young man, no older than 30.

"I was born in Lubumbashi," he said, "the only son of devout parents, Catholics in religion. I observed the church and recommendations of my parents concerning God and salvation from my earliest years. When I was about twenty years old, being influenced by the "holy-spiritual and holy-scriptural" preaching of the Pentecostals, I joined their community. I loved studying Holy Scripture, and devoted myself to that with enormous zeal. I believed myself to have found the true church and thought I should strive to help others on the difficult path of salvation. My seniors expressed their pleasure with my zeal for learning and religious work and quickly promoted me to be a pastor of a community.

Shortly thereafter another, higher step awaited me. They gave me the chair of teacher and preacher for a very large area, which included all of Lubumbashi and its environs. I dedicated myself to preaching the Word of God, and did so not just zealously but fanatically. I thought myself fortunate because I was above others and could lead them wherever I wanted with my interpretations of Scripture. I spent two years visiting parishes and guiding pastors with my fiery sermons. I never hesitated to speak to people in authority, and it was I who converted the Governor of Lubumbashi from Papism to Pentecostalism, as well as various other people.

"One day as I was reading the New Testament I noticed that we did not observe certain tasks, teachings and messages that Christ had given to

His disciples. For example, He gave to the Apostles and their successors the power to bind and loose sins (Jn. 20: 22-23). In the form of bread and wine He gave to commune of His Body and Blood for eternal life. He commanded them to baptize the followers of the new religion, etc. All of this roused many questions in my heart, since my sermons failed to take these commandments and promises of the Lord into account. I grew uneasy and began to wonder: "Maybe the religion I follow is mistaken and I am walking on the road of delusion?" Until I would be able to answer these questions, which troubled me so much that I was unable to sleep, I decided to stop preaching and leave without saying anything to anyone.

"I went to Kolwezi and rented a straw hut and did a bit of commerce, just enough to secure my food each day. I stopped going to churches, even though the neighborhood had over thirty different churches. I would, however, pray thus: "My God, I know that you left one true Church behind on the Earth. The Pentecostals and others have told me that the early Church has ceased to exist. Yet, how then can one explain Your words, 'the gates of Hell shall not prevail against it' (Matt. 16.18). Your Church exists then, and is one. Enlighten me that I may recognize it and follow it."

"I didn't cease day and night to carry out this one work: prayer for God to reveal to me His Church. Two years passed without receiving an answer or confirmation of any sort. Thoughts of disbelief encircled me. Clouds of despair enveloped me. But God in His goodness saw my distress and was not slow in revealing to me what I desired.

"One night I saw in my sleep a person, unknown to me, dressed in black. It was a European wearing a black cassock and with a long white beard, his countenance was peaceable and affectionate and his eyes full of love and compassion. He approached me and spoke to me in Swahili. I wondered, how is it that old man, being a European, knows Swahili? He told me word for word the following: "I am Saint Nicholas. If you wish to be saved follow my Church." After blessing me he immediately disappeared.

"I got up in a state of amazement and wondered who this white priest might be who knew Swahili and which Church was his? Who would be able to take me to this Church? I went out and started asking passers-by to which Church does Saint Nicholas belong. After a good few days of fruitless investigation, God sent me His envoy: an Orthodox Christian woman from the parish of St. George in Kolwezi who had heard about my enquiries and was overjoyed to supply answers to my searching. She led me to Father Iakovos who lives there, and Father Iakovos brought me to the Mission here today."

Such was the tortuous route whereby this young man found peace, in the bosom of the true Church who is the Mother of all of us. "How great is our God!"

The young man attended catechism with humility and eagerness up to the day of his baptism. He reads Orthodox books with holy zeal, prepared to serve the Church as a priest in the future, if it is God's will, as he told me. Towards his former pastors and teachers among the Pentecostals, he maintains a friendly but struggling stance. He creates serious doubts about the existence of truth in their community. He confides in them the wondrous event of his sudden change and entrance into Orthodoxy. In this way, a light of Christ has started to shine in the spiritual darkness of the African jungle.

A month after our meeting, the young man came to see me again to tell me how he was progressing in his new path in life and here is another incident he described to me: "One evening as I was reading the Epistle of St. James, I suddenly felt a light fresh breeze blowing round me. It entered into me and filled my whole being with joy and spiritual stillness. It was the first time I had ever experienced such holy feelings. At the same time I could hear a voice saying: 'Abandon all the heresies and follow the Orthodox Church unhesitatingly.' Father, I have no doubt that I now belong to the true ancient Church of Christ. I praise God for the fact that the Orthodox Church is present here in our town, so near us. I thank you, the apostles of the Lord, for coming to our country. Pray for me to follow you for the glory of our Christ."

He was baptized under the name of Nicholas and currently lives in Lubumbashi, working there for God in the bosom of His Church.

A Double Healing of an Anemic Girl

A great deal of humanitarian work goes on at the Orthodox Mission's clinic in Kamanyola, at our Monastery of St. Nektarios, which is adjoined by the girls' boarding school. Here I would like to draw attention to just one miraculous incident.

A little girl called Kalumbu was a serious sufferer from anemia. Her older sister, Calliope, who had been baptized long before with her grandmother, tried to explain things to her little sister, who was still unbaptised. Hearing the news, as her final wish Kalumbu asked to be baptized.

Father Iakovos came and baptized her as she wished. Kalumba took, as her new name, Anastasia. The miracle is that, as soon as she was baptized, Anastasia was both physically and spiritually healed. She arose from her bed and asked for something to eat, and a few days later was discharged from the clinic. Since then Calliope and Anastasia have maintained close relations with the Monastery of St. Nektarios.

The Archangel Michael in Kolwezi

We were in the middle of the harvest season, June, 1996, in the village of the farm of the Mission, Louankoko, and the parish of St. Kyrikos.

During this period, Christian women from Kolwezi had come for the corn harvest. Among them was Paraskevi. She is a tall, modest, humble and pious Orthodox Christian from the parish of St. George in Kolwezi. Her chief and defining characteristics are simplicity and humility.

She was then suffering from a sore throat so bad that for one whole week she wasn't able to speak at all. Only by a slight whisper could she communicate with others. He throat was in terrible pain and she was praying to the Archangel Michael to come to her aid. During the months of June and July in Kolwezi it is very cold, almost reaching freezing temperatures.

On Monday, June 15, 1996 I arrived at the farm. All the women came to greet me. Paraskevi greeted me without speaking.

The next morning, before setting off to work, she was among the first who came to greet me. Her voice was clear and strong. "I'm very well today," she tells me. "My throat opened up completely and the illness has gone." And she went on to tell me how during the night she had seen a white saint with a white beard in a black cassock, who asked her: "Are you sick?"

"Yes, I am."

"From now on your illness is over. Go and tell Father Iakovos."

Paraskevi replied: "There is no Father Iakovos here, only Father Damaskinos."

The Saint said: "Go and tell him to read, carefully, the first Psalm of David and the first two verses of the First Epistle of St. Paul to the Corinthians, chapter 15." Then he departed.

When Mama Paraskevi told me all of this, I wondered how she was able to remember so many numbers and words that the Saint had told her. I also asked her: "Which saints have you been praying to since you have been ill, and why?"

"I pray to the Archangel Michael, because in 1986 I gave birth to a boy who was baptized under the name of Pachomios. That year he was seriously ill and close to death. One night a European woman came up to me and said: 'Take your child to the Archangel Michael.' I replied, 'I don't know who he is.' The woman then said: 'Look! He is the one standing over there. Go over to him and tell him what you need.' I went over to him and knelt before him and placed my child in his arms. He blessed the child and stroked him and gave him back to me healed.

I woke as if from a coma. Full of agony I went to see my child. He felt better. Shortly thereafter he was completely well."

A Miracle of St. Nektarios and St. Anastasia of Rome

St. Nektarios of Aegina

The wife of our priest Fr. Lazarus, Maria Ikosa, fell sick with high blood pressure (Ta.28) in 1991 and was miraculously healed by St. Nektarios.

The illness returned to her during the night of 28th of October 1996. Her body even became rigidly stiff with it. On the 29th Father Lazarus came to see me to report her state of health. I sent the Fathers to pray for her and to ask for the intercession of St. Arsenios of Cappadocia and of St. Anastasia of Rome, as this is the date of her commemorative feast day. The icon of this Saint was included among the icons they took with them.

That night Maria saw the following vision in her dream:

"A white girl came to me in my sleep dressed as a holy Martyr. She took me by my hand and said: 'I see that you are sick, but I cannot make you well without the blessing of the Bishop.' At that moment a Bishop enters in who seems to me to be Saint Nektarios. I believe it was he because he lives close to us, his monastery being located only two hundred meters from our house. The young Martyr Anastasia then takes my hand and inserts an injection into my left arm. Then Saint Nektarios approaches me and asks three times: 'Are you healed?'

And I answered him, 'Yes.'

Then the Bishop asked me: 'In whose name have you been healed?'

'In the name of Jesus Christ,' I replied.

Then I said to the Saint, 'Don't leave, holy Bishop. Wait for me to make you something to eat.'

He then told me, 'I would like to rest for a while.'

Deacon Lazarus who was next to me said, 'Here is a bed where you can rest.'

Then Deacon Daniel entered the house with his wife and said: 'Are you sure you want to have the Saint of God rest in your bed? Isn't that disrespect and impiety toward his Person?'

The Bishop told him: 'No, I'll sleep here, because this house has the blessing of God.'

Indeed, he rested a while. The food was then ready and we all sat down to eat. After the meal I addressed the Bishop and said: 'Don't leave, holy Bishop. I want to give you something like a memorial gift from your visit to our house.'

Then the native Nun, Thekla, suddenly appeared beside me and said: 'Give him the icon I brought you back from Greece.' I gave him this icon, the face of which had an excellent brilliance and shone brightly from luminous rays that were fluctuating.

Saint Nektarios took the icon into his embrace and said to us: 'May my blessing and her blessing be with you always.' And then he left."

Sacred Artifacts Rescued from Fire

In the village of Tshipaya, where one of our parishes is located, our catechist one day suffered a misfortune. His thatched house was reduced to ashes, because of a fire he had lit to warm the house and on which to cook. Everything he owned was destroyed. Among the ashes, though, he found a number of items intact, and was surprised that they had somehow managed to be saved. He found a New Testament, a wooden cross and a prayer rope, all unharmed by the fire. In this way, in saving these sacred objects from the fire, God gave him great comfort in his misfortune.

Go to the Orthodox Church

In the middle of the month of September, 1996, one of our priests accompanied the pregnant wife of one of our workers to the maternity clinic. There he met and spoke with the doctor and director of the clinic who was Roman Catholic. The clinic belongs to the Methodists. After a brief conversation with regard to the matter at hand, the priest, out of courtesy, invited the director, whose name was Mouagkala, to visit our Orthodox Church.

Before, however, he could arrange such a visit he was the recipient of a succession of mysterious night-time invitations and within three days had placed a call to the Mission Center. A meeting was arranged for the upcoming Sunday with the head of the Mission, Hieromonk Meletios.

After their discussion Father Meletios sent him to me, telling me: "Talk a while with the good doctor and whatever he needs give it to him." Having greeted him, I asked him to tell me about himself and his life. He told me the following:

"I work as the director of the Methodist Maternity clinic. I am a Roman Catholic and I came here today to learn something about your Church. It is the first time I have ever entered an Orthodox Church."

"How did you come to be interested in our Church?" I asked him.

"Father, the following incidents recently happened to me. For three consecutive days now, although asleep, I hear a voice that tells me repeatedly: 'Go to the Orthodox Church, go to the Orthodox Church.' I couldn't stand it any longer, so I called and came over to meet you."

"God loves you," I told him, "and takes care for the salvation of your soul. Take these books and once you finish reading them come back to see me and we'll answer any further questions you might have. Afterwards, you can take other books as well."

He returned again and again, many times. That, however, which moved him the most and propelled him to decide to become a catechumen of the Church was the showing of videotapes of Litanies with the Incorrupt Relics of the Saints of our Church, such as Saint John the Russian, Saint Spyridon from Corfu, Saint Dionysios of Zakinthos and others. He was amazed and greatly moved by this supernatural phenomenon of the incorrupt bodies of our Saints.

He was baptized, with his wife, who is also a doctor, and his six children on the Feast of Theophany of 1998. A friend of his, a professor of literature, together with his entire family followed him into the Church as well. May God bless them with eternal life.

Our Orthodox Faith Reaches Distant Sandoa

Since 1993 a new parish is "under construction" in the distant town of Sandoa. That which is of great interest to us is just how our true Faith became known there.

That year the Mission had sent a Zairian priest, Father Romanos, to visit his relatives there. When the other residents saw him with his black cassock and his beard, they asked him who he was and to which Church he belonged. He answered them and they in turn, at the prompting of the Holy Spirit, asked to learn more. In the end, the Faith that Christ brought to the world was revealed to them.

The first to show interest was a bank employee, a Protestant. He gathered information and then went to Kolwezi to meet Father Meletios. He subsequently took with him some reading material for catechism and some icons and returned to Sandoa. He began his great missionary work with uncommon zeal. He attracted 250 catechumens to whom he gave intensive instruction based on all he was reading. He extended his ministry of the word to two other villages and urged the catechumens to build their own churches themselves, in the provisional way, which is the norm, made of bricks with grass roofing. All this work was completed within the space of two years. Father Meletios visited them to help them to embark on their new spiritual life. They underwent the appropriate preparation, and in October, 1994, 250 catechumens from three parishes were baptized.

Liturgy in the open air, under the expanse of the African heavens.

Adventures in Pastoral Work

One week before Christmas in 1994, the Mission sent Father Romanos to Sandoa, some 450km from Kolwezi, to celebrate the services of the twelve days from Christmas to Theophany.

During the journey he fell seriously ill with malaria and spent the night at the house of Father Cosmas, the village priest of Kawayongo. On the following day they continued, with difficulty, their journey to Sandoa. They arrived but it proved impossible for Father Romanos to perform his priestly duties. They sent us a message asking us to send them a vehicle as quickly as possible to transport Father Romanos back to Kolwezi as his condition was very bad.

The Mission sent the nurse, Sister Xenia, with two others to Sandoa. It was the rainy season and there was a lot of mud on the road, which had become a running river. They arrived after a journey of eighteen hours and incredible difficulties. As Sister Xenia later told us, the car had become submerged in water up to its frame many times and became stuck in the mud twice. In Sandoa the newly baptized Christians and the 200 catechumens brought to the Faith by the zeal of the catechist Timothy, were waiting and greeted them with great warmth. They helped Father Romanos and then left again straight away without even taking any food for the journey. So ended this "odyssey" in the Zairian jungle.

Better to be Poor and Orthodox than Rich and Heretical

In the village of Luena, 300km from Kolwezi, we have a parish dedicated to the Twelve Apostles. The parish catechist there is one Joachim, who was a teacher at the Methodist primary school until 1993.

The Methodists had pressured him to enter their "church" on pain of losing his job. But Joachim, an Orthodox Christian worthy of his Faith, preferred the loss of his job with all the consequences that this entailed for his family, in order to keep his Faith. He left the school and began working in the forest making wood charcoal to sell as a means of upkeep for his four children. He has now opened an Orthodox primary school, where he has gathered Orthodox children, and the Mission pays them frequent visits to help with the administration.

Blessed are you Joachim! Jesus Christ will never abandon you, for you are one of the greatest confessors of the Orthodox Faith today in Africa.

Better to be Poor and Orthodox than Rich and Muslim

In total, the catechists at the Orthodox Mission in Kolwezi number nearly 150. The Mission does not pay them but it does provide help with their material needs, in the form of medical supplies and other things.

The catechist of Fungurume was given the opportunity to get rich, but he rejected the proposal. Muslim "missionaries" had offered him the chance to become one of their catechists with a salary ten times that which a priest of the Mission receives. But with courage and the decisiveness of a confessor he thus eluded this satanic trap. He remains poor and a worker in the fields, as before, but holds tight the treasure of the Faith that the blessed Father Cosmas delivered to him.

Blessed are you too, brother Panayiotis! The grace of Christ will never leave you, for you have not spurned God in favor of mammon!

Baptismal Testimonies

Maximos Bulungo

"I live at the Mission boarding house for boys and also study at the Mission's school. For over one year I was given catechism instruction and then was baptized at Pentecost in 1996. I took the name of Maximos in honor of Saint Maximos the Confessor.

"Before stepping into the water I was afraid and ashamed to be standing in front of all the people around me. Yet, when Father Meletios baptized me and I ascended the stairs of the baptismal font, the shame and the fear left me. I felt much joy and lightness in my heart. Before, I had had something heavy on my head, which, after the baptism, left me as well.

"At the hour of Divine Communion, when I took the Body and Blood of Christ within me for the first time, I felt a warmth throughout my body and heard a voice within me saying: 'You've found salvation in this Faith.' I even began to pray within me with great ease. I thank God for the great gift He has given me, the sinner."

Timothy Kakwata

"I am a student at the Intermediate School of the Orthodox Mission. I was catechized for more than eight months and was baptized at Pentecost in 1996. At the baptism I took the name of Timothy.

"After my baptism I felt a tremendous joy within. My heart became light within me. I sensed that I was now a true human being. The love

Father Meletios during a recent mass Baptism in Kolwezi.

of God entered my heart and now I love God very much, for He led me to the true Church."

Gregory Saega

"I was baptized in 1992 by Father Meletios. I thank God for His goodness in setting me on the right path of Orthodoxy, the path of true gladness. Orthodoxy is the Church that has kept the Tradition of the Holy Apostles and Fathers, unchanged, until today. Glory to our All-good God!"

Emmanuel Ngandu

"I am a student at the Intermediate school of the Mission in Kolwezi. Before I was baptized, under the direction of Father Meletios, I confessed for the first time in my life. I felt something like a weight leave from my heart. On Saturday, June 8th 1996, I was baptized together with some other friends and fellow students, taking the name of Emmanuel. I felt as if this body of mine left and another, new, clean and lighter body took its place. Inside of this new body I feel now my own paradise.

"I even felt that my face changed and this world in which I had lived until then left me. A new world entered in and taught me how the life of a true Christian ought to be."

Damaskinos Kalenga

"I am a student at the Orthodox Mission in Kolwezi. I was baptized at Pentecost in 1996 and took the name of Damaskinos.

"I felt within me an unprecedented change. I felt that which someone feels who was locked up in prison and then set free. Such freedom I felt when I came up out of the water! My whole body and heart were washed in a lake of indescribable joy and internal lightness. The weight that oppressed my heart left forever. It fell away just like scales falling from a fish.

Since my baptism I feel that my life is under the guidance of the Holy Spirit. I recognize Who it is that dwells in me and Who it is that governs me. When I was a pagan idol-worshipper I didn't know how to distinguish between that which is evil and that which is good."

Christodoulos Muchaila

"I work as a tailor for the Orthodox Mission of Kolwezi and am the brother, according to the flesh, of the great-schema nun, Thekla.

"I was baptized on the 8th of June 1996, taking the name of Christodoulos. When I emerged from the water I felt a lightness and divine power within my heart. My soul felt that from then on the Holy Spirit was guiding it. I feel that I have become a new man and unmurmuring in the Name of Jesus Christ. Now I pray to the Holy Trinity to enlighten other people who still haven't come to know the Orthodox Church; that He will bless them to be baptized and experience that which I've lived as well. I express my thanks to Father Meletios who guided me to Christ and to my sister, the nun Thekla, who catechized me. Glory to Thee, O God! Amen."

Meletios Mazeze

"I am a student at the Intermediate school of the Orthodox Mission in Kolwezi. I glorify God for having helped me to recognize the true Church and true Faith.

"Before being baptized I didn't know to walk the true path. When I began attending catechism classes and began to chant in church my soul, little by little, began to rejoice and beg me to faithfully follow the lessons and services of the Church. I still had an inclination toward the fleshly sins. After my baptism I felt a major change within me. I took the name of Meletios. My body prodded me to sin with women, but a voice within me prevented me, saying: 'Don't do that, it's a sin.' I have much joy for this great act of love that God showed me. I always thank Him for it. My desire is to become a co-worker of the Mission in the work of spreading Orthodoxy throughout my country. Glory be to God for all things!"

Despina Yav

"I am a student at the Intermediate school in Kolwezi. I was baptized at Pentecost in 1996.

"After my Baptism, I felt great joy in my heart and when I emerged from the water, my body had become completely weightless. My family, and especially my sister's husband, said that my face was like that of a little girl's, even though I am 19 years of age.

On Sunday, the day after my baptism, a fellow Christian stopped us and said: 'Despina, your face has changed and your voice is new.' Deep within, however, I don't know how this change happened. A few days later, when they showed me the photograph from the baptism I was astonished, for my face had a spiritual light and an unfamiliar change. From then until this very moment, as I write these lines, I have within my heart only joy. My soul calls me to go every day to the church. Nearly every Sunday I approach and commune of the Holy Mysteries, when once again my heart is filled with inexpressible joy. Such joy I had never experienced before in my life. The illumination that I sometimes feel pour over my face is without a doubt the Grace of the Holy Spirit.

This love for the Church moved me to become a novice in the Monastery of Saint Nektarios of our Mission. I hope that throughout my life I can live intensely the mystery of love of our Christ. May it be the will of God that I become a nun! I seek it and, as a gift of God, I await it from His hands. Amen."

George Kasongo

"I was baptized in 1995 on the Feast of Theophany together with my wife Marianthi and my children Christina, Irene, Nicholas, John and Theano. I took the name of George. I am an English teacher at the Mission's "Light of Christ" Farm School in Kolwezi. I received my spiritual instruction about

The author, with priests and children of the Mission.

the true Orthodox Church first through the Headmistress Mrs. Efterpia Ilias, and then from our Archimandrite Meletios, who taught me that man couldn't find salvation other than in the bosom of the Church of Christ and not outside it. At first I was a Roman Catholic, then I went to the Protestants and finally I entered forever the Orthodox Church.

"The principle, that salvation can only be found within the Church, I had already heard when I left the Roman Catholics. One day a Catholic priest had also said that nobody will find their soul's salvation if they remain Protestant to the end of their life. So, I decided like Joshua to join the true Church along with all my family and to serve God in the bosom of the Orthodox Church. I even brought my sister-in-law who was baptized under the name of Despina Yav Kabey, along with the rest of my family.

"After baptism I felt great joy throughout my soul and body. My whole body was released from its heaviness and became very light. This joy gives peace to my soul. I can't describe this joy so as for other people to understand and feel it. I felt as if a fire had been kindled in my heart and a love of always going to church. Inside I love to pray, chant and hear the hymns of our Church.

In my spirit I see our Monks as Angels when they celebrate the Liturgy. The devil hates this joy and provokes temptations for me. But God helps me to struggle. I never felt this joy in the other 'churches' I attended before becoming an Orthodox Christian."

Silbestros Kambashi

"I was baptized in 1996 on the Feast of Pentecost at the age of 14. Father Meletios gave me the name of Silbestros.

No one from among my family is Orthodox, but neither has anyone prohibited me from entering the Church. I entered the Church on my own, without anyone telling me about it. I like it more than the others. I like the Fathers who labor here, for I haven't seen or heard of any misdeed of theirs. I am grateful to them for they teach me with their example. And furthermore because they have traversed oceans and countries in order to be here with us and bring us the true Gospel of Christ.

I believe in the Holy Trinity and the Holy Mysteries of our Church, by which I hope to be saved. I pray to Jesus Christ, the King of all the world and Judge of the Universe to protect all of you who have come here to help us. I was regenerated in the Orthodox Church and I will die Orthodox. I don't have anything else to write. I thank God that I am Orthodox."

Author's note: This child lives at the boarding school of our Mission. He is distinguished for his amazing academic progress and his love for the Church and Her Divine Services. His desire, as he told me, is to study law and to work as a statesman of his country for the propagation of the Orthodox Faith.

The Missionary
Association of

SAINT COSMAS AITOLOS

Publishers of the
Greek Editions of
APOSTLE TO ZAIRE

AVAILABLE FROM THE ASSOCIATION:

IERAPOSTOLOS OF ZAIRE	ST. COSMAS AITOLOS	TRUE ACCOUNTS FROM THE
FR. COSMAS GRIGORIATIS	QUARTERLY MAGAZINE	ORTHODOX MISSION IN AFRICA
224 PAGES * $16.00 (1,500 DRS)	SENT FREE TO ALL INQUIRERS	140 PAGES * $5.00 (2,000 DRS)

KONSTANTINOPOLEOS 30 * STAVROUPOLI - THESSALONIKI, 564 29 GREECE
Tel. (3) 031.606.920 or 031.602.602

*All those who desire to support the work of the Association financially
may do so by depositing their donation into the following bank account::
#235/296004-49 at the National Bank of Greece.*

This 2nd Edition of

Apostle to Zaire

written by Demetrios Aslanidis & Monk Damascene Grigoriatis, translated by Fr. Peter Alban Heers is typeset in Baskerville and printed in this two thousand twenty second year of our Lord's Holy Incarnation, with 1500 copies printed on fifty pound Natures weight paper, available from Uncut Mountain Press: translators and publishers of Orthodox Christian theological and spiritual literature. Find the book you are looking for at

www.uncutmountainpress.com

GLORY BE TO GOD
FOR ALL THINGS

AMEN.

www.ingramcontent.com/pod-product-compliance
Lightning Source LLC
Chambersburg PA
CBHW041343060526
44323CB00011B/5